C000196671

HILLFORTS OF NORTHERN WALES

Michael Senior

ISBN: 0-86381-959-1

Cover design: Sian Parri

First published in 2005 by
Gwasg Carreg Gwalch, 12 Iard yr Orsaf, Llanrwst, Wales LL26 0EH
01492 642031   01492 641502
books@carreg-gwalch.co.uk   Internet: www.carreg-gwalch.co.uk

CONTENTS

A Glossary of Welsh place-names

Holyhead	–	*Caergybi*
Anglesey	–	*Ynys Môn*
Denbighshire	–	*Sir Ddinbych*
Severn Valley	–	*Dyffryn Hafren*
Usk	–	*Wysg*
Holy Island	–	*Ynys Gybi*
Holyhead Mountain	–	*Mynydd Twr*
South Stack	–	*Ynys Lawd*
Red Wharf Bay	–	*Y Traeth Coch*
Puffin Sound	–	*Swnt Seiriol*
Great Orme's Head	–	*Penygogarth*
Orme	–	*Y Gogarth*
Dee	–	*Dyfrdwy*
Flint	–	*Fflint*
Menai Strait	–	*Afon Menai*
Snowdonia	–	*Eryri*
Pembrokeshire	–	*Sir Benfro*
Bardsey Sound	–	*Swnt Enlli*
The Marches	–	*Y Gororau*
Halkyn	–	*Helygain*
Oswestry	–	*Croesoswallt*
Offa's Dyke	–	*Clawdd Offa*

INTRODUCTION

There are many things to be said in favour of pursuing this apparently endless but absorbing task of trying to understand, and to know about, our predecessors in this land, but the one that strikes me now is the pleasure of exposure to our inspiring landscape. The hillforts, by their nature, stand in magnificent locations, perched, in many cases, on commanding hills overlooking rich patterns of fields and hedgerow trees spread out below them like maps, usually with all-round views; in some cases seaward facing on the edges of promontories and cliffs. Because generally elevated and often remote, they are part of an old landscape which has, in most cases, remained unaffected by urban intrusion. They are as if designed to make you aware of the magical complexity of the landscape of northern Wales.

Here we have a distinct phenomenon, and a distinct period of time, just as in a previous book I found that a certain culture and a certain level of social development were involved in the setting up of those equally distinct phenomena, the standing stones. High on their mountain slopes, they also often stand in breath-taking positions, but compared to the hillforts they are as a whole almost diffident.

Just as in the case of the standing stones, so the northern Welsh hillforts give us this chance: to consider the circumstances and aspirations, from their evidence, of a people far remote from us in time, but not in space – since they lived right here, where we live, within our view, the view we see every day. I hope to use these artefacts, the hillforts, as I tried to use the stones, as a convenient route into their lives.

There are so many of them that a sampling system will be necessary. I can see two out of the window now, without moving at all from my keyboard. If I moved a bit I could see two more. Looped in a broad arc around the mountain heartland of northern Wales, between the extremities of Holyhead and the finger of the Llŷn peninsula on the one hand, and the border country of the Clwyd and Ceiriog valleys on the other, there are today the remains of more than a hundred of such defended enclosures. Thirteen of these are of over fifteen acres in size, forty of them over three. It is hard to know where to stop, because the chain (for such it seems to be) goes on into Shropshire and central-Wales.

It will be noticed that I have already begged a number of questions. Firstly, to talk of them as 'forts' and as 'defended' (as everyone does) is to make an assumption about their type of use, which is in fact the main subject which we should be investigating. Secondly, we have, by the act of counting them, put them all into the same category, whereas it should at least be considered that they are of different forms, and so perhaps made by different people under different conditions.

Many of the authorities refer with admiration to the Ordnance Survey's map of 1962, *Southern Britain in the Iron Age*. In our area there are marked five 'finds of Iron Age material', and all the other entries are 'Hillforts and Similar Defended Enclosures' – the subject of this book. In other words we have to face the fact that what we know about the way of life of the population of Iron Age Wales must be derived almost entirely from these rings of wall, ditch and embankment, and from such items as have been found within them.

The Ordnance Survey breaks these 'hillforts' into the two main categories of **univallate** and **multivallate**, that is, according to whether they have one or more ramparts. It then further divides these groups according to their size. The larger forts, of which there are thirteen in our area, they identify as those of over fifteen enclosed acres. Of these larger ones only

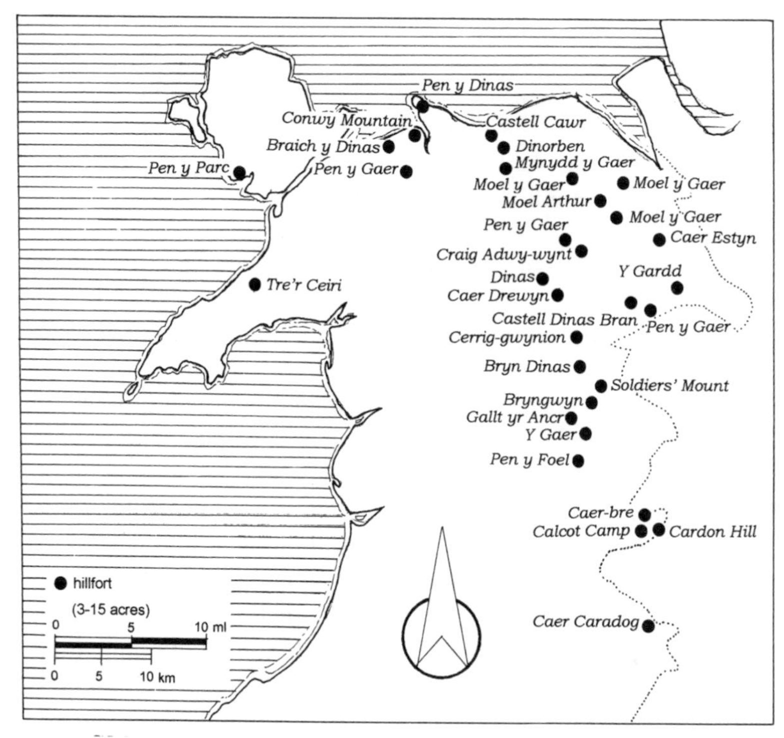

Medium-sized Iron Age forts in northern Wales

five are of the single-walled type, the remaining eight having double ramparts. Enclosures of between three and fifteen acres form the Survey's next category, and in this group in northern Wales there are no less than twenty-eight, some of them so close together that they almost overlap on the map. Here again there are more (eighteen, if we go down into Shropshire) with more than one wall, than there are with only one. Of all the forts over three acres, the pattern shows a thick chain of multivallate examples running through the Clwyd valley, giving way further south to a more loosely spread band of univallate enclosures flowing down the border.

The works enclosing *under* three acres are too numerous even to count. They jostle the greater ones on the map like moons around a planet, but showing no regular pattern, sometimes in clusters, sometimes in isolation.

In general, of all the forts over three acres, Anglesey, as an area, has the fewest: two of each type; Llŷn has three univallate, and, if you count Dinas Dinlle as being in Llŷn, two multivallate – though in the lesser category, under three acres, it has more of the 'multi' than the 'uni' type. Along the northern coast there are four examples of each, and down through Denbighshire and along the Cheshire and Shropshire borders, thirteen of the enclosures of over three acres have more than one wall, and the same amount have one.

There is some point in making these distinctions even at this very early stage, as they may well turn out to be of importance to us in this present investigation. One of the theories put forward by archaeologists and by the Ancient Monuments Commission is, as we shall see, that single-wall enclosures were a first response to an inward migration, and at a later time were re-occupied, perhaps by those immigrants, in the face of further arrivals, when further encircling rings were added.

Another possible way of distinguishing the types of forts is

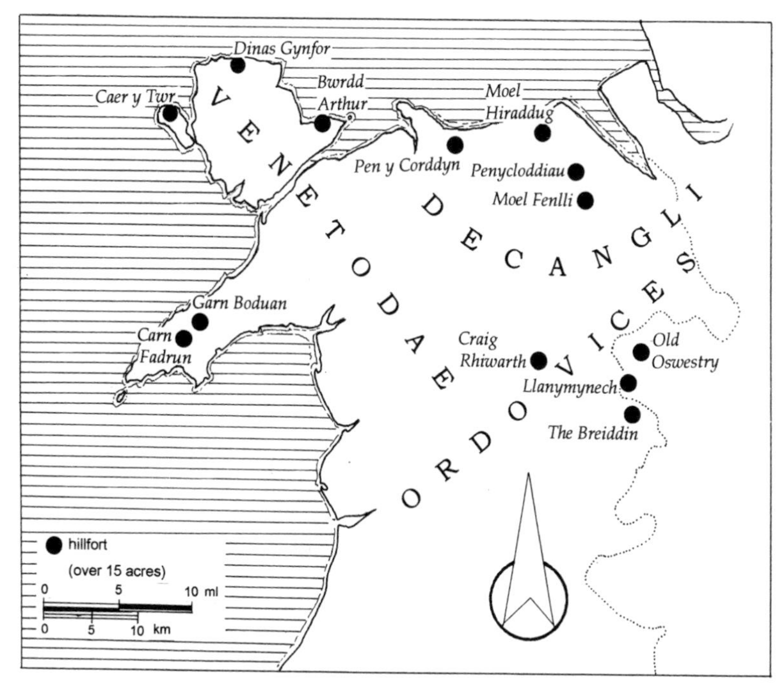

Large Iron Age forts in northern Wales

the division between those with, and those without, interior huts. The Ancient Monuments Commission Inventory for Anglesey, for instance, divides them this way – finding there to be a roughly equal number of each type. This is perhaps not the significant distinction which it might at first appear to be, since it should not lead us to suppose, at least with any confidence, that some of the forts were permanently inhabited and others not. Turf huts leave no residue at all when they decay, and the only evidence of huts which we might expect to find are those which were better (more durably) built – with a round, levelled floor, and the familiar circle of a stone wall-base. It might be argued that the absence of these identifiable structures indicates a lack of long-term settled population. But a settled population could presumably also live in short-term but endlessly and easily renewable turf huts; and in general we must say that the lack of evidence of huts should not be taken as proof of the absence of inhabitants.

Finds of artefacts are a different matter.

Unfortunately, very few of the northern Welsh hillforts have been fully excavated, and those several, which have been partially so, were investigated some time ago (in some cases in the 19th century) and so perhaps not under modern rigorous archaeological conditions. Finds from all these have been disappointingly sparse, though where they can be dated they are of crucial interest in the light they shed on the circumstances of occupation of the hillforts. Two forts which have been subjected to full investigations were the subject of rescue excavations ahead of their destruction by quarrying – so that in effect we know much more about what is no longer there than about what is. Since the forms of these now vanished forts are so clearly identifiable as being the same as the ones we can still see, it would be fair, I think, to generalise from these few examples, and in the chapter below where I deal with dating, and in that dealing with the question of purpose, I shall make extensive use of these records, backed up, as they are, by the partial, sporadic, finds elsewhere.

One thing we know for certain about the hillforts (as with the standing stones) is that they are where they are, and in seeking to understand them we shall have to pay careful attention to this factor. It at once becomes apparent that they have a tendency to form chains in fairly close proximity, for instance along the slopes of the Clwyd valley overlooking the river, or, in westerly Gwynedd, up the winding river Llyfni.

In the next chapter, so that we may know what we are dealing with, I am going to set out a general description of the forts of our area and their locations and peculiarities. We may then take a detailed look at the best examples of each type, in each area. The archaeological finds and the matter of dating will occupy a further chapter, as will a survey of the background of the people of the time.

Sufficient information may by then be available to us to enable us to form some sort of conclusion.

One

A PATTERN OF LAND-USE

It would be hard to be on top of a hill in northern Wales and not to be in sight of the sea. Perhaps we should rather remark on the fact that this can be achieved – by penetrating inland far enough along the river valleys; some of these though, like the Conwy estuary as viewed from Pen y Gaer, are in fact themselves inlets of the sea. That the hillforts have a coastal pattern about them is of no surprise. This is a coastal place.

Rather more interesting would be to see what relationship, if any, they have to each other. Here no pattern readily emerges, since any initially apparent tendency to form an even spread across the surface of the land is contradicted by the proximity of Tre'r Ceiri, Garn Boduan and Garn Fadrun, on the Llŷn peninsula. Of these three univallate forts of over three acres, the two latter are large, in the sense of being over fifteen acres. There are other noticeable pairs, obstructing any idea of even spacing. Conwy Mountain and Pen y Dinas, on the Great Orme, are just under four miles apart, as are Penycorddyn, above Llanddulas, and the now destroyed Dinorben. In one or two cases, a small fort occurs in such proximity to a larger one that there seems to be some connection, as if the one were a subsidiary outpost of the other. This seems to be clearly the case with the fort on the summit of Conwy Mountain and that on Allt Wen, its western extension; and Pen-y-gaer and Caer Bach in the Conwy valley seem to be similarly connected by the fact of their proximity.

In general, though, the distances between the forts vary directly with their size. The larger forts (with the Llŷn exceptions) are mainly over five miles apart, and twenty miles divide the nearest Anglesey large fort from Penycorddyn – but there are many lesser instances in this case in between. The lesser forts cluster thickly, particularly away from the coast in the river valleys.

Although the forts usually occupy hilltops, occasionally the ends of spurs or ridges, and only infrequently are set on lumps of coastal cliffs, even the relatively elevated ones are not located at any great height. There are exceptions to this, three of which stand out. Foel Fenlli, on a steep-sided dome above the Clwyd valley, rises to 1,500 feet, as does the wonderful citadel of Tre'r Ceiri. These are clearly mountain outlooks rather than hilltop ones, as was at one time that on Penmaenmawr. Caer Bach (at 1,300) and Dinas above Llanfairfechan (1,200) are high as well, but clearly have not sought the greatest eminence in their area, since they are overlooked by higher slopes and hilltops all around them.

As it turns out, the inaccessibility of at least Tre'r Ceiri and (we may speculate) Penmaenmawr's Braich y Dinas is counterparted by an exceptional density of occupation level and an extensive period of use. Tre'r Ceiri, for instance, has the remains of a hundred and fifty huts, and finds have indicated that its use went on until the end of the 4th century AD. That is, well into the period of the Roman occupation and so throughout it. There is plentiful evidence, as we shall later see in detail, that a period of intentional destruction of the hillforts occurred: probably, we can reason, in the autumn of the year AD 77.

Late that summer, an event had taken place which shook the complacency of the Roman army which was then colonising Britain. Somewhere in northern Wales (and this is not the right place to wonder where) a party of Roman cavalry out on a field exercise was ambushed and slaughtered by members of the tribe of the Ordovices, in whose territory they were. This was a blow to general morale, fragile enough anyway in an always potentially hostile country, worse in the mountainous region where the Roman military machine proved cumbersome and hampered. It happened, by one of those chances of history, that the governorship of Britain had just been taken over by Agricola, a man of such a temperament as would not incline him to preside over a faltering army.

It had been assumed that it was too late in the year to begin a campaign, let alone one in the northern Welsh mountains. The troops were already dispersed to their winter quarters. Agricola, however, acted decisively, and so perhaps took the hill tribes by surprise. He mustered the Roman forces and set off at once into the mountainous homeland of the Ordovices. There he "cut to pieces almost the whole fighting force of the nation", and to do so, of course, he would have had to assault them in their hillforts.

We know from an earlier passage in Tacitus that the Romans had already had some experience of attacking these hillforts. Ostorius, an earlier Governor, had led the army into the Severn valley to confront the resistance under Caractacus. "On one side there were steep hills. Wherever the gradient was gentler, stones were piled into a kind of rampart." When the Romans reached the ramparts, they had a problem: "in an exchange of missiles, they came off worse..." They had the disadvantage, of course, of having to attack uphill. They resorted to one of their most effective techniques, the *testudo* (literally a tortoise): "...under a roof of locked shields, the Romans demolished the crude and clumsy stone embankment". Tacitus, of course, had not himself seen the elaborate gatehouses and well-built wallwalks of some of our fortified hills, and he writes from reports supplied by the conquering side.

We know from examples elsewhere that when the hillforts were demolished the natives were relocated to a lowland valley site, where they could be more easily controlled: at Maiden

Castle, for instance, where the inhabitants were moved down to Dorchester, and on the Wrekin in Shropshire where they were resettled in the Roman town of Wroxeter, and nearer to home, in southern Wales, the Silures were brought down from their hillfort to the north-west of Usk to form part of the Roman civil settlement of Isca. There is evidence, we shall find, that in some cases they were permitted to retain the use of their hilltop homes, or perhaps came back to them when the Roman presence became weaker, but impotently now, without the benefit of protective walling.

If then places such as Tre'r Ceiri, which went on being used throughout Roman times, and possibly the perched defences on Penmaenmawr, were proof against the might of Rome, because not even under the *testudo* would the legionaries dare to struggle up such a hill, with a barrage of stones raining down on them: then why, we may wonder, were not more forts built on our plentiful high mountains? In the distribution of the forts (which is largely the subject we are dealing with at present) the pattern shows a notable avoidance of the higher heartland. They noticeably seem to be concentrated on sites overlooking lower regions. Yet Tre'r Ceiri had been able not only to defy the invaders (if indeed they knew of it at all) but in doing so to act as home for a time at least to a population amounting to a tribe.

I am going to suggest that this was because withstanding an invasion by an army such as that of the Roman empire was not a purpose for which the forts were designed. Perhaps it was not even, for a start, the *sort* of thing that they were intended for. Indeed, when most of them were founded, such a cataclysm on such a scale could not have been envisaged at all. Thus it was that, initiated in times of lesser danger, most of the more easily assaulted defences fell to Ostorius, Suetonius, and Agricola. They were not really (it turned out) defendable, at least not against the *testudo*. Retreating to Tre'r Ceiri and Braich y Dinas may have seemed, and may have been, the only option.

One thing we may note, while now surveying the characters of the forts in general, is that by the nature of their siting (on the tops of prominent hills) they are visible one from another. That is to say, that from each of them you can clearly see another one, and, with the exception of those obviously at extremities, this applies at least two ways: there is always one visible in each direction.

The land in between is thus viewed by them, and reciprocally, those on that land in between can view them. There is, in the valleys and on the coastal plain, always a hillfort above you within sight. This is perhaps too early a point in our investigations to start forming conclusions – before, that is, we have had a chance to look at the datable evidence and such as we know of the conditions of the time, or times, of the long period of use of the hillforts. But we may at least note at the start that they were all in proximity to cultivatable land. That the land around them was actually cultivated at the time is at least likely, from the plentiful examples of hut systems in the areas outside the forts being connected with terraced fields. There is ample evidence from parts of England (perhaps less well established in Wales) that some forts at least were associated with prehistoric field systems. James Dyer's helpful little book, *Hillforts of England and Wales*, gives the example of the Maiden Bower plateau fort in Bedfordshire, surrounded by acres of elaborately bounded fields.

Many of the huts of course have, and had since Bronze Age times, enclosures alongside them, such as could be used for corralling stock. The point is that stock farming is a more flexible activity than arable farming, and more easily protected in times of trouble, being more readily mobile. Since the land was cultivated in Iron Age times, and not just grazed, a more elaborate system of ensuring political and social stability was required. This is not a speculation, not a 'what if' or 'would have' form of history, since stability is not an option in terms of agriculture, but a *sine qua non*.

We can say at least that the coastal plain and the river valleys where the forts are all located are both suitable places (unlike the upland hillscape and the moorland wilderness where there are none of them) for arable cultivation. It does not follow logically of course that their existence is causally related to this fact. If at least we could show that the choice of the locations reveals no other purpose – such as, for instance, the setting up of a border, or the exercise of control over a trade route – then the fact that they do all overlook such a terrain might help towards an explanation of their purpose.

Two

WALLS, BANKS AND DITCHES

Looking in detail now at some specific examples in our area, it will help us to understand their relationship to each other and the thinking which went into them, if we bear in mind some features which hillforts have in common. It is a matter of overlap of common features, in that not all forts have any set of them complete. Some have an inner wall and an outer rampart, some just a single ring of stone. Some have a v-shaped ditch between two lines of defence. Some have an elaborate gateway, some just a gap. Some have a guardhouse or gate-hut inside the entrance. Almost all that are made of stone have signs that the walls were once well-faced, and those which are better preserved have the remains of a recognisable wall-walk.

It will be convenient for this survey to divide northern Wales into sections, a process to which it is quite amenable, and to take a sample of forts from each. Anglesey is a natural unit, and with its own geographical nature likely to reveal individual characteristics in its artefacts. Likewise the Llŷn peninsula, in its own way isolated and separated from the coastal plain, is likely to display in anything it produces a tendency to focus on the sea. There is a marginal region at its neck, which merges in land-form with the coast opposed to Anglesey. The hillforts skirt the mountain heartland, running along the northern coast and looping into the Conwy valley. What appears to be a separate and distinct concentration of them emphasises the border nature of the Clwyd and Ceiriog valleys. The fact that they seem to fall into groups may of course be misleading, may be simply a function of our regional geography.

At once you are struck by the extreme range of these people. They got to places hardly anyone would go to now. Perched out at the end of Holy Island, for instance, on Holyhead Mountain itself, stuck out in the tideways of the Irish Sea, **Caer y Twr** is in a wild place now, exposed to seaboard gales, and one cannot imagine that such a spot would ever have been hospitable. A single, well-defined rampart runs round the northern half of the summit, the most prominent feature of which is its entrance in the north-east corner, flanked by more heavily built, inturned wall-ends. Unusually, one looks down from this ancient outlook not onto the green Welsh farmland so familiar from other fortified hills, but onto the vast breakwater and harbour of the port of Holyhead. This striking fact underlines the sea-facing nature of these forts. They appear to be more concerned with water than with landward neighbours.

Caer y Twr lies at 720 feet above sea level and covers 17 acres. Like so many of these forts, it uses the natural sharpness of the land as a defence on two of its sides, the south-east and the south-west. Although the enclosed area is fairly level, it is at the same time rough and craggy, and one cannot imagine that it could ever have been thought a good place to build habitations. Indeed, there are no signs of any, but hut-circles are frequent in the surrounding countryside, and a terraced area outside the northern wall seems to have been levelled for such a purpose. The hut group and terracing near Tŷ Mawr, on the road running up to South Stack, the group known as Cytiau'r Gwyddelod, 'the Irishmen's huts', lie just under a mile away to the south-west. These, which have been excavated and dated to the Roman period – that is, occupied in the 3rd and 4th centuries – may well be associated with the great enclosure on the mountain.

Caer y Twr was evidently well-constructed, although its

single wall shows no sign of an external ditch. It is set on the crest of the slope, and incorporates in its line outcrops of natural rock which form potential look-out posts with views both ways along the wall. For a stretch in the north, parts of a wall-walk may still be seen, a levelled platform some three to four feet off the ground, which again is detectable at one point in the east, indicating that the whole structure was much more elaborate and sophisticated than one would guess at first glance. A long, levelled hollow runs up to and through the entrance, well into the interior of the fort, suggesting that perhaps the compound was designed to be accessible to wheeled vehicles. There is clear evidence at one point on the north side that the wall has been breached and cast down. The Romans came to Anglesey in 61 and 77 AD, though there is no reason to suppose that they penetrated as far as this at those times. They built their fort at Caergybi (now surrounding the town's church) at a later phase, in the third to fourth centuries AD, when Segontium had declined in strength and it became necessary to protect Anglesey (and perhaps its valuable copper deposits) from sea-borne raids, a time when the huts at Tŷ Mawr and elsewhere were still in use. Perhaps it is to this time that we must date the pulling down of a crucial part of Caer y Twr's defensive wall.

About the same size and also single-walled, lying at a diametrically opposite point of the island, the fort known as **Bwrdd Arthur** or **Dinsylwy** is of a very different character, due mainly to a rounder, gentler and somehow more spacious terrain. The top of 'Arthur's Table' is flat, and although the slopes fall from it steeply, it is not protected anywhere by cliffs, unlike the fort at Holyhead, so that it was evidently felt necessary to encircle completely the whole thing. Dinsylwy affords remarkable views in two directions, down to the sweep of Red Wharf Bay on the one hand, and out past Puffin Sound across the bay to the coast at Llanfairfechan and the Great Orme's Head in the other.

The wall is well-built, making use of large limestone blocks set upright and filled between by packings of smaller stones, like the limestone walling at the Iron Age village of Dinlligwy, near the north-east coast. There are in this case two entrances, one at the south side which is clearly well constructed, and a smaller one on the west. Inside the fort, a number of huts have been found, and Roman coins and Roman-period pottery indicate a period of use, again, during the third and fourth centuries.

Anglesey has other, lesser forts, two of which are notable for their position, being of the form, unusual in northern Wales, of defended headlands. These are also positioned at opposite corners of the island, this time in the north and the south, so that Anglesey is in effect squared off by the four main coastal forts, west, north, east, and south.

The one that lies at the extreme north end, a promontory fort known as **Dinas Gynfor**, is not far from the village of Llanbadrig, in an area of deep and ancient tradition. Reached down winding single-track lanes, dense with gorse and bracken (in the view, now, the inevitable wind-turbines on distant hillsides), it lies at the edge of a land humped and lumped by geological complexity. An early medieval nunnery apparently stood beside the cove at Llanlleiana, and you cannot help feeling that even then that this was an anciently inhabited land, now long reverted to wilderness and become, in its very essence, remote. The little bay has an air of secrecy, as if suitable for use by pirates, and was in use as a harbour for loading and unloading goods until comparatively recently. From the headland above it, on which the hillfort stands, the view is of wild coastal extreme, in the normal state of which a white surf pesters the cliffs and coves beneath you. The lines of defence of Dinas Gynfor are, now, vestigial, visible as a long straight mound on the south-west, landward, side, and sporadic piles of white stones which do not look as if they have ever been formed into a wall but may be connected with the "irregular quarry-ditch" mentioned by the Inventory. Dinas Gynfor, unlike so may of the forts, strikes us as being very much on its own, and although Holyhead Mountain is visible, it is distant, and the familiar Anglesey panorama of the Snowdonia mountains is from here, so far out on the northern edge of the island, only a line of peaks without foothills.

At the opposite corner of the island, at Llangadwaladr, another promontory fort, **Trwyn y Parc**, consists of a massive rampart across the headland's neck. It lies in the romantic world of the Malltraeth Sands, and is not viewable because it is on closely protected private land. But one can see at a glance that this part of Anglesey has such extensive views that it is clear that the whole stretch of hillforts between Tre'r Ceiri and Penmaenmawr would be visible from here; and the headland itself protects a landing place at the side of the bay watered by the Afon Cefni.

LLŶN

Similarly, not strictly a hill-fort, but rather a cliff-top outpost, directly across Caernarfon Bay from Trwyn y Parc, on the mainland, the vast mound of **Dinas Dinlle** has for a long time been falling into the sea. Its summit standing at barely a hundred feet above the water, it has little outlook except that along the uninspiring shore, and so is regarded as an example of a fortification controlling a convenient landing place. It makes use of a pre-existing glacial deposit, a prominent outcrop in a largely low-lying, once marshy, area, and it seems from what one can see of the beach side that its two ramparts (once encircling it, now broken in half) are composed of rounded stones, whether by sea or ice, two elements which meet and overlap on this silted coast.

There is a single entrance on the south-east side, and within the level area surrounded by the banks are the signs of huts and enclosures. It seem that in the 18th century there was more to see. Pennant notes: "Within are the remains of buildings, of an oblong form, constructed with earth and stones; and in one part is a tumulus of the same materials." Such few coins and bits of pot as have been found show Dinas Dinlle to have been occupied in Roman times, the 2nd and 3rd centuries AD.

Legend suggests an older connection, but legend is of course often retrospective. There is, though, undeniably something about the Mabinogion story of Lleu Llaw Gyffes (told in the fourth branch *Math son of Mathonwy*) which suggests an ancient provenance, as if its heroes and heroines are the disguises worn, in Christian times, by native deities. It is known as Dinlle because this is the fortress of Lleu, who was brought by the wizard Gwydion to confront his mother Arianrhod, 'walking along the seashore between there and Aber Menai', to her castle off the coast which may now be seen as a reef of stones from the top of Dinas Dinlle at low tide. "Then they came towards Dinas Dinlleu. And then Lleu Llaw Gyffes was reared..."

It is no surprise that a story such as that of Lleu should get attached to something as monumental as Dinas Dinlle. One would have expected something of the sort to occur at **Tre'r Ceiri,** town of the giants, but it is not specified in lore who these giants were. What one feels about Tre'r Ceiri, as it happens, is not mythic or monstrous at all, but rather it conveys something poignantly human. Alone among the northern Welsh hillforts, and probably to a greater extent than hillforts anywhere, Tre'r Ceiri is much as its inhabitants left it, unslighted, unpillaged, uneroded by time. You feel their presence around you. You feel almost embarrassed to be there, as if you have wandered into their town while they were out, and at any moment they may come back.

Its remarkable state of repair points to the importance of this hillfort for our understanding of the condition of the others. The Romans evidently did not pull it down. We know that they had a major outpost at Caernarfon, less than fifteen miles away, and a camp at Dolbenmaen, which seems to have been their furthest penetration into Llŷn. If Tre'r Ceiri's height and the steepness of the slopes onto which it looks down made it out of reach of the testudo, or if perhaps its remoteness made it seem to the Roman commanders irrelevant, we have here two things to marvel at. One is the realisation of how thorough and effective was the Roman policy of pulling down the hillforts, since this is the only one still intact. The other is the thought that here something of the independent, unrestricted habit of thought and way of life survived, to carry forward into Llŷn and Eifionydd and the future, a recognisable spirit of undiluted Welshness. If it was the imposition of Roman order on western Wales as a whole that started the process of settlement and lines of communication, which laid the infrastructure for Wales's absorption into the greater European world, then it was because something evaded this at Tre'r Ceiri that this process was less complete than it might have been.

Not much has been found at Tre'r Ceiri datable from before the mid-2nd century AD, and its use is attestable from evidence up to the 4th century, that is, the time when Roman troops were withdrawn from Segontium to go to Gaul with the usurping Emperor Magnus Maximus, in 383. These dates tie Tre'r Ceiri again to the presence of Rome in northern Wales. It was perhaps not felt necessary to live at such a defendable height before the march into the Welsh heartland by Suetonius, in 60 AD, and Agricola, in 77. The fort at Caernarfon became more used after 140 AD, when the occupation of Tre'r Ceiri seems to have flourished, and by the time the last artefacts were left there, in the late 4th century, it had perhaps become safe to come back down.

Another feature which supports this interpretation of the role of Tre'r Ceiri in reaction to the Roman occupation is the large number of huts within the compound. Some hillforts have none, as we have seen, some only a few, indicating that these were not intended for use as permanent settlements, but only perhaps as refuges in times of trouble or as safe storage for reserve supplies. Tre'r Ceiri has within it some 150 huts. They cluster in beehive-like complexes, as if groups of people (for instance an extended family) wished to live together. These groups of huts are more or less evenly spread over its 950 by 340 feet extent.

Archaeologists do not speculate. We, on the other hand, are free to draw conclusions from the evidence with which they provide us. From the datable finds at Tre'r Ceiri, it seems that it came to be inhabited some years after the other datable hillforts fell suddenly out of use. We may guess then that at least some of its 150 huts provided a refuge for people from other areas who, through luck, cunning or determination, somehow evaded the iron grip of *pax romana*.

Pennant reported finding the traces of three walls, but the lowest of these (which he described as 'very imperfect') is not a wall at all, but the remains of compounds or other works well down the slope. A partial outer wall does span some of the slope half way up the mountain on the north and west sides, the inevitable line of approach. The track up the hill leads to a gateway in it, set out of line with the major gateway in the upper wall, indicating a defensive purpose. It is this wall which is most impressive, running as it does round the whole summit of the hill, here on the north-west side where one approaches it towering above you thirteen feet high and at these more accessible points up to fifteen feet thick. On inspection, the wall-walk may be seen to be formed by the raising from the flat top of the wall of an outer parapet, about three feet high.

There are two main entrances, both approached by cleared tracks, the one at the south-west end approaching the fort through flanking walls, then entering by a long narrow passage through strengthened ramparts. The one on the western side seems by the width of the approach track to have been the major entrance, though it is slightly less elaborate in form.

On the highest point of the enclosed summit of the mountain (one of the three peaks of Yr Eifl), at 1500 feet, itself a superb outlook, there remains a cairn which probably predates the elaborate Iron Age structure surrounding it by a thousand years. This is perhaps significant, and it will not be the only time we have reason to wonder whether what we see now of these Iron Age forts are perhaps the successors to hilltop works originally stemming from the Bronze Age. Alternatively, of course, it might be sheer coincidence that the summit of this mountain was thought to be a worthy place to site a burial a thousand years before it became a suitable defensive position.

The huts which cover the surface of the enclosed area vary considerably in form and size. Some are round, some D-shaped, some egg-shaped, some surprisingly almost square, suggesting the aping of Roman style. Finds of Roman-period pottery are much more frequent in these more rectangular huts, indicating perhaps that they were a later development, and indicating a sequence from simple round to D-shaped, some subdivided, and finally square. Archaeologists are so reliant on pottery that it is a distinct inconvenience that it seems that the earliest people to live in this district were not pottery-users. Such as has been found indicates a period of use from the mid-2nd century until the 4th. There have been no post-Roman finds at all, indicating that Tre'r Ceiri had no after-use once its major defensive role became obsolete.

A lot of the huts are about twelve to twenty feet wide. Besides the remarkable cluster of structures inside the fort, there are signs that huts, as well as compounds, dotted the hillsides outside the walls.

Many of the huts within Tre'r Ceiri were archaeologically excavated extensively by Harold Hughes in the early years of the 20th century. What is perhaps most remarkable about this is the general paucity of finds. As the Ancient Monuments Inventory puts it: "...in the extensive clearances at Tre'r Ceiri only about one hut in five produced datable objects, and these were seldom more than sherds from a single pot in each hut". One factor may be that long before the investigation reported in the *Archaeologia Cambrensis* in 1904, the huts of Tre'r Ceiri had already been given a thorough (but unprofessional) going over. About fifty years earlier, an old woman in Llithfaen, at the southern foot of the mountain, had dreamt that a copper cauldron full of gold was buried in Tre'r Ceiri. "This unfortunate dream did more harm to the cytiau [huts] of Tre'r Ceiri than many centuries of natural causes of decay."

The early archaeologists found the huts 'crudely built', not a characteristic that particularly strikes us today, used, as we are, to seeing many much more damaged remains. They tried sheltering in one from a northerly gale, but the wind penetrated the fifteen foot thick walls and forced them "to seek a less draughty retreat". The huts, they found, were paved on a foundation of rubble, a fact sustained by the later excavations. This paving kept the floor dry, since water accumulates easily in any hollows on the peaty soil below, which itself lay on a bed of impervious clay.

A few huts were investigated again in 1939, over four days in March, and more fully in 1956. Archaeologists reliably tut-tut about the antics of their predecessors, but it seems in this case that Harold Hughes had more success in practical terms than did his successors. In the words of A. H.A. Hogg, writing up his fifties investigations in the Archaeological Journal for 1960, "no evidence for actual dating was found in 1939 or 1956, but some deductions can be made from the finds made during the 1904 and 1906 excavations…"

Among the rubble of one of the huts "were found some scraps of burnt bone and a small fragment of a shale ring, the only artifact discovered during the excavations." This fragment is only an inch long, and "of no value for dating purposes".

Perhaps part of the reason for the lack of finds by 1956 was that the site had already been very thoroughly gone over, not just by professionals but by anyone else. The 1956 excavations were notable for the extent of damage revealed, the report sighing sadly that the interior of hut after hut had been "destroyed by a treasure-hunter's pit." Moreover, it comes to the rather surprising conclusion that the state of Tre'r Ceiri in general, as it is now, is affected precisely by the extent to which it has been investigated: "It should be noted that the present condition of the huts, and what at first sight seems to be their very remarkable state of preservation, is usually the result of excavations, either those made by Harold Hughes or others which have never been recorded." What happened was that, in digging out the interiors, the excavators piled stones up on top of the walls. "This has at least the merit of giving a fairly close indication of the original height of the huts, but unfortunately the walls on to which the stones were built were sometimes the creation of the workmen, and the present plans of the huts do not necessarily represent their original form."

In other words, Tre'r Ceiri is by no means as undisturbed as your first impression of it might lead you to suppose. Nevertheless, Hogg says that Tre'r Ceiri is "probably the best preserved of all the hill towns of southern Britain, and certainly can give a better idea than any other of the original appearance of a place of this kind."

It is remarkable (given the lack of huts in many hillforts) that another, which has within it about 170, as compared to Tre'r Ceiri's 150 or so, lies just over five miles away, and so supports any conjecture we might posit for Llŷn's having been a refuge from the Roman advance.

Garn Boduan is surrounded by trees, but out on top, the hut circles are obvious and impressive. On the summit, within the main fort, is a smaller fortress, conspicuous because it is better built, with a well-dressed outer face. It has its own approach from within the main walls along a sort of shelf, flanked by steep crags. Another entrance, at the western side, has been carefully blocked, like the north-east entrance of the hillfort itself. Steps up to the rampart imply that a wall-walk once topped them.

Within the smaller fort are the remains of two huts, which have been excavated, revealing finds of small fragments of "very crude pottery", of which it is said (in the Inventory) that it was "unlikely that it would have come into use until Roman pottery had ceased to be available", which seems to have been the basis for the dating of Garn Boduan as post-Roman. Some beads, which could be of any date after the 1st century, and a fragment of the rim of a large grinding bowl, which might be 2nd century, were also found.

The hillfort itself is reckoned to be of two periods, the northern side of the defences having been excavated in 1954. The first period is represented by a mainly rubble rampart best preserved in the north-east, with no sign of a gateway. The second period rampart is larger but similar and better preserved. It still stands in places to a height of five to six feet and is still faced in places. Six huts lie between the earlier and later walls. Of the two entrances, the main one on the south-east was approached by a revetted track, and the second on the north-east has been, like one in the smaller fort, deliberately blocked.

Garn Boduan means the 'residence of Buan', who was a son of Llywarch Hen, a sixth century prince, Buan himself being allocatable to the first half of the seventh century, so that it at least remains possible that the small fort was a response in dark age times to the dynastic troubles of north-western Wales.

So close to Garn Boduan as to seem right next door, the defences at **Porth Dinllaen** are, however, of a different sort. This is a promontory fort, like those on Anglesey, and like those as well, apparently intended to protect a useful landing place. Indeed, the bay which the headland protects is the best harbour on this coast, which was the main reason it was for a time favoured as the official port for Ireland. To an early trading nation it would have been invaluable, and the fort of Trwyn Porth Dinllaen needs no further explanation. It was also an easy headland to defend, skirted by cliffs and being long and narrow, so that all that was required was a line of banks and ditches across its neck. About 130 feet of its western half may still be seen, more evident as a ditch than a bank, and much of its original line has been interfered with, since the road to the beach passes through it.

One cannot but be impressed by how densely defended Llŷn was. Less than four miles from the major fort of Garn Boduan, travelling south, is the major fort of **Garn Fadrun**. This is an extreme sort of place, the last prominent mountain in Llŷn, surrounded on all sides by its rough coastline, yielding, from its summit, an encapsulating view into and out of northern Wales. You see the great ranges of the Snowdonia mountains in one direction, and the Pembrokeshire coast in another. You look out westwards to Anglesey and Holyhead, and occasionally beyond them to the hills of Ireland, as if Garn Fadrun itself is an outpost in the Celtic Sea.

A sharp-sided conical mountain, rising to over 1000 feet, Garn Fadrun is exhilarating to climb and well worth the effort.

On the summit, the remains represent, it is thought, two phases of defensive works: a small fort followed by a much larger one. Many huts, some making use of the earlier ramparts, cluster around the west side of the hill. On the slight evidence of their similarity to those on Tre'r Ceiri, and the even slighter evidence for the date of those, they are assigned to the late Roman period. Only a few lie within the enclosure formed by the larger rampart, but many – possibly hundreds – of huts dot the slopes around, outside the ramparts. As at Tre'r Ceiri, the summit was the site of an earlier burial, in the form of a now ruined cairn enclosing a Bronze Age cist, near the middle of the inner rampart, the coincidence again, it is thought, of the Bronze Age custom of locating important burials on the peaks of mountains with that of the later period's use of the same sort of mountains for defence.

There are signs that both walls, inner and outer, were once well-faced: one stretch is still visible north of the summit, though elsewhere the inner ramparts seem to have been occasionally removed to form the outer, which is still largely intact. The gates are hard to distinguish now, but zig-zag approach tracks on the north and south sides indicate the probable main points of entry as being at both those ends.

There is another structure near the summit, on the west side. A stone wall here forms the base of a small fort, which, it seems almost certain, is that referred to by Giraldus Cambrensis in his *Itinerary*, the record of his journey through Wales in 1188. Two stone castles, he said, had been recently built: one in Eifionydd called Deudraeth, and "the other named Garn Madryn, the property of the sons of Owen, built on the other side of the river towards the sea, on the head-land Lleyn". Garn Fadrun came back into use, it seems, in the troubled times following the death of Owain Gwynedd.

Whether it is evidence of the density of population of Llŷn in

Iron Age times, or perhaps a symptom of a reaction to the imposition of Roman presence everywhere else, there are yet more hillforts to be found on the peninsula besides the great and extensive examples just visited. Only a further seven and a half miles further south is the neat round double-banked enclosure known as **Castell Odo**. It forms a ring around the top of Mynydd Ystum, not far from the end of the peninsula, Aberdaron, and Bardsey Sound.

Castell Odo is unusual in being quite small – it measures about 170 feet in diameter – and, at 480 foot above sea level, it is not specially elevated, but it has the highly characteristic feature of a sublime and inspiring outlook. The barely distinguishable banks which make Castell Odo's summit into something of a plateau are more visible on the western side. Its slopes are gentler than those of many of Llŷn's forts, and one gets the impression it would be a place quite easy to overrun – hence perhaps the various episodes of its apparent failure as a defended spot.

Castell Odo is unusual in having been fully excavated, in this case by Dr. Leslie Alcock, of the University of Wales, in the summers of 1958 and 1959. Some of the results are important for the understanding of the history of hillforts in general.

Alcock came to the conclusion that in its earliest form, the settlement on Mynydd Ystum had been undefended. It consisted of a few huts, and dated from the first phase of the Iron Age. Finds from this phase indicate, according to the investigator, a date as early as about 425 B.C. This village (as has apparently happened elsewhere) was later encircled with a wooden stockade, perhaps to keep wild animals out, or domestic animals in. In this case, Alcock judged this to have been uncompleted, and the original settlement then caught fire. Some time later, the hilltop was surrounded by a low bank, on the line of the present outer rampart. This, in due course, was later reinforced with stone, and the inner rampart (also stone-built) added, though finds from both these phases are very rare, and later non-existent, so that dating is impossible.

The walls appear to have been intentionally pulled down, but even after that the site continued to be in occupation.

Alcock's conclusions (published in the report of the work in *Archaeologia Cambrensis*, in 1960) are avowedly tentative and his ultimate reading of the evidence is ambiguous. What seemed clear the first year, he says, had become doubtful by the second. The original timber buildings are inferred from apparent post-holes, and these are taken to be primary because they are overlaid by others. But no artefacts were found except for fragments of pottery, from "large coarse jars" which "may have been used principally for storing grain" or perhaps for cooking. Cooking undoubtedly went on, evidenced by signs of fires and numerous animal bones (too broken to be identifiable) and teeth, probably of cattle.

The crudeness of the pottery and its poor quality make it comparable to 'Flat-Rimmed Ware' which belongs to the end of the Bronze Age. But fragments of one large storage jar show that it "clearly belongs to the Iron A ceramic tradition", which is to say "at least as early as the fourth century B.C." It is the only example in northern Wales, although Iron Age A pottery is occasionally found in southern Wales and the Marches, but there, it is unlike the Castell Odo example. On the basis of these fragments, much is then surmised: seaborne colonization is likely, since no links inland are shown. The extensive use of timbering itself is uncharacteristic of the northern Welsh hillforts, and may, he suggests, indicate the arrival of new people. It seems curiously stubborn of them to insist on following their traditional building style, even in treeless Llŷn ("Deforestation of the sea-girt and wind-harried promontory must have begun at an early date...") instead of imitating the locals and using the plentiful stone all around. But Alcock insists that they did this: "The use of timber for houses, and especially for a stockade which would have required some thousands of feet of thick straight posts, argues that these were the work of invaders from some well-wooded region, who had not yet adapted their building techniques to the exigencies of north-west Wales."

The first settlement does not appear to have been long-lived: sherds come from a very small number of vessels. Alcock shows that it was destroyed by fire, more explicitly stormed while a defensive stockade was still unfinished: "On the west of the perimeter part of the stockade had already been erected, while in an immediately adjacent sector only the topsoil had been removed on the line of the projected defence. Around the north-east not even a marking-out trench had been dug." He had no doubt that the stockade had been burnt, along with the huts within it. "All the packing stones were found to be heavily burnt, and the palisade trench contained several pockets of charcoal which were probably the remains of the original posts."

After that, a thin layer of rain-washed soil covering the remains of the stockade indicates a short period of abandonment, which was followed by a new structure, at first a simple piled-up rampart, more an enclosure than a defence. Only "indeterminate" finds occur from this period, such as cannot even be securely dated to it. Alcock concludes that pottery played little part in the native tradition, which ("undetected in the archaeological record") made use of vessels of wood and leather – pottery being introduced from outside by invaders. The next phase of use of Castell Odo was still an enclosure, such as would "keep domestic animals in and wild animals out", rather than a military fortification. Its entrances, for instance, were undefended. But then why, one wonders, would it have needed to be on top of a hill?

During this period the use of a double bank and of dry-stone revetments points, he thinks, to an Iron Age B culture, but there is one thing missing which casts doubt on this: very few slingstones were found, "less than a score", and the slingstone is for the people of Iron Age B something of a trademark: "the characteristic and indestructible evidence of their methods of warfare and cattle-herding..." It is this which makes him consider that the double banks were not for military purposes, though their obvious application to sling warfare makes one wonder whether there is some other reason for the lack of the stones.

After a fairly long continuous occupation "at a low level of material culture", the banks were deliberately slighted, their revetments demolished either side of the entrance, "and all the large stones removed". A new road was driven through the entrance-way. It must be said that this apparent act of demilitarization does not tally with the enclosures having been a civilian rather that a military post.

At any rate, it now continued to be in use but in an open form. We might be inclined to see in this the Roman campaign of the 2nd century AD, but there is the problem that this would raise more questions than it would settle, such as 'why Castell Odo?', since there is no other evidence of Roman penetration into farthest Llŷn.

Alcock's hypothesis that this was nevertheless what occurred is based on his inability to think of anything else. "At the same time it is difficult, if not impossible, to believe that any purely local tribal body possessed the power and organisation to carry out the systematic demolition that was perpetrated at Castell Odo." The reason for the lack of Roman finds, he supposes, is that they demilitarised Llŷn and then withdrew, to leave it unadministered as tribal territory. Evidence for the continuing occupation during Roman times is, however, slight: it consists of the fact that a saddle-quern (by means of which corn is ground by rubbing a pebble on a long stone with a concave upper face) was used as building material, though in good condition, which indicates that it had become outdated with the introduction of the rotary quern, that is, a system in which one stone rotates against another. This seems likely to have come about as a result of the Roman occupation.

There is what appears to be a rectangular hut on the very top of the hill, which reminds one of the early medieval fort on Garn Fadrun, but it is concluded in this case that this is not a building at all, but simply a long low mound of the sort known as 'pillow mounds', which seem, rather surprisingly, "so far as the evidence goes, to have been artificial rabbit warrens."

To summarise Alcock's conclusions, to which we must pay heed in view of the rare occasion of a systematic investigation: a very early, small and isolated pottery-using group of colonists set up a sort of farmstead in what they took to be peaceful conditions on this mild coastal conical hill near their landing-place, perhaps before anyone else had penetrated this extreme region of Llŷn. They suddenly found the need to defend it, but before they had succeeded in doing so, were overrun, and the whole thing torched – one assumes by an expanding population of previously native inhabitants of the inland area. These non-pottery users, shortly after, occupied this desirable site themselves and remained in control of it for a considerable time, only partly being affected by the Roman occupation of Wales.

This format became an accepted pattern in the thinking of students of hillforts – the taking over of a site by the process of one group driving out another – and so is a pattern which has been assumed elsewhere; but it must be said that in this original case, the whole supposed sequential structure is built on the basis of a few fragments of a large jar, and the lack of any further ones. This is exciting, in other words, because it arises (for once) from a detailed investigation; yet it is also tantalising because it could so easily all be wrong.

In many ways quite unlike the examples we have been studying, and more like some of those in Anglesey (because a cliff-top, rather than a hill-top, fort), is **Pared Mawr**, south of Llanengan. This is most notable for the breathtaking view of the bay of Porth Ceiriad to the east and the shoreline far below, and the clear-watered blue and green sea. You come up into the small fort over its steep ramparts and you are greeted there by a guaranteed shock. It was not apparent, walking across the level land, how high up we are here; nor would you ever have guessed, in this gentle landscape, how sheer is the fall of the cliffs to the rocky shore, how extreme a sort of place this is, in fact, and how distant from the tamed world. This stretch of coast is one not many on land have ever seen, and it lies on no obvious sea-routes either. It strikes you as a profoundly secret place.

CENTRAL ZONE

As we move along the coast towards Conwy Bay, the view to Anglesey predominates to start with, and shortly after that, towards the Orme. From the Llanfairfechan coast we can look across towards Bwrdd Arthur, the fort above Red Wharf Bay with its two directions of view. Here, above Llanfairfechan, the fort called **Dinas** on a 1,200 foot plump round prominence looking out so widely over its own private landscape, enclosed by the even greater uplands, revealed within its modest enclosure the remains of fourteen huts, and many hut-groups, enclosures and field systems have been found within sight of it for instance across the valley of the Afon Ddu around the hill known as Garreg Fawr. This is, we feel once again, an old and much-used landscape. At Dinas, as so often elsewhere, it was evidently not felt necessary to defend the steepest side, and in other areas the ramparts, once doubly encircling the round hill, have been extensively robbed, no doubt to build those long stone walls which still line and texture the uplands. Excavations were carried out in 1925, and a hut excavated which showed the remains of a hearth, a posthole – which presumably housed a support for the roof – and some fragments of querns, presumably of the 'saddle' variety (though this is not stated) since they had with them the remains of rubbing stones.

Whatever the purpose of siting Dinas where it is, one cannot help feeling that it would have become redundant, since it is towered over by Penmaenmawr, where once, before they took the mountain away, was one of the largest and most substantial hillforts in the area. Did that, then, perhaps come later? Was it at some point felt necessary to move to a higher (and so of course less convenient) place of refuge? Everything that could be seen from Dinas could better be seen from the summit of Penmaenmawr above it, so that we have to imagine Dinas, here, as being either a sort of offshoot or outpost or, more likely, surely, a precursor, of the greater defence-works there.

The fact that the hillfort on Penmaenmawr known as **Braich y Dinas** is no longer there is an unfortunate irony since it was, throughout history, not only one of the greatest but apparently the best preserved of the forts, and as it turned out, one of the most fully investigated. Indeed, it occurs in an early source for this area, the document known as the 'Ancient Survey of Penmaenmawr', supposed to have been written by Sir John Wynn of Gwydir in the early 17th century (but more likely someone else's notes on something Sir John had written). In fact, only a small part of the pamphlet has anything to do with Penmaenmawr, but such as it is, it establishes that the 'Dinas' as they called it, was an object of awe to the first antiquarians.

"When ytt stood," writes the author, it "was ympregnable". It was "the ultimum refugium, the strongest, surest, and safest refuge and place of defence that the ancient Brittaynes had in all Snowdon, to defende themselves from the incursions and inrodes of there enemyes". Just who these ancient Brittaynes were, or when, he is unclear about, since he relates the "Druids'Circle" nearby (itself nearly two thousand years old by the time of the druids and of these Iron Age forts) to the same period of use as the 'Dinas': "ytt shoulde seeme that this was a place whereunto the ancient Britaynes came from the Dinas aforesaid to encampe themselves and trayne there souldiers". This early historian has a complaint which we may share: "ytt is greate pitty that our Britishe histories are so ymbeseled that we have noe certeynty for these things, but must onely rely upon tradicion".

Pennant, in the 18th century, likewise went to see for himself this remarkable feature of which he had read the account attributed to Sir John. He found three 'if not four' walls, rising distinctly one above the other, one which he measured standing at nine feet. Many small circular buildings lay randomly between the walls. He observed a well cut into the rock, which was constantly full of rain water. He noted the similarity of this stronghold to those on Llŷn.

We are a bit better off, today, as far as the facts are concerned, even though we can no longer get to see the ruins for ourselves, since the quarry has taken the whole of it away, along with much of Penmaenmawr mountain. The site was thoroughly excavated between 1911 and 1922 by Mr. Harold Hughes, whose findings are recorded in *Archaeologia Cambrensis* and summarised in Bezant Lowe's *Heart of Northern Wales*, Volume II.

Massive ramparts of roughly coursed rubble masonry rose, as in Pennant's day, to nine foot high, between eight and fifteen feet thick. Hughes reckoned there were ninety 'or more' huts, mostly oval in shape. A plan by W.G.Haslam shows about 150. Many of the huts lay between the ramparts as well as within them, and all were east of the summit ridge. More than eighty of these were investigated by Hughes. Remarkably, the datable finds all fell between 100AD and 400AD, that is, during the Roman period itself. The fact that there were saddle querns for grinding corn, but none of the rotary type, throws doubt on the extent to which the settlement here was influenced by contact with the Romans.

There were three cairns on the summit (perhaps the structures Pennant identified as 'towers, or cells'), a central one at the top, and the well was still identifiable when Hughes did his digs.

The 1911 dig found, besides the usual grain-pounding stones, a bronze pin, said to be of the La Tène type (that is, of the later Celtic immigration) but of Roman workmanship, and some pottery similar to that found at Tre'r Ceiri. In 1912, some fragments of iron objects were found, and in 1914, an iron ring, a nail, and portions of a bronze torque, among other less significant items. In 1921, many more huts were excavated, and a silver bracelet found. In 1922, thirty-five huts, mainly between the ramparts, were dug, and it turned out that the richest sector of the population apparently lived there. The shells of mussels, periwinkles, limpets and cockles, and the tooth of an ox, as well as the grinding stones, indicated a mixed diet. There was evidence of fires within the huts, and a fragment of a cooking pot of grey buff ware with a rolled rim, datable to the first part of the second century, and a rim of a Samian vessel identifiable as early 2nd – a type of pottery common in Roman sites, so called after the Greek island of Samos, which yielded the reddish clay from which early examples of this much-copied form of ware were made. Some pieces of amphorae (that is, I suppose, the remains of wine jars) were judged to have been of Roman origin, perhaps a discarded vessel from Segontium or Canovium. Moreover, there were Roman coins among these exotic items on this part of the hill. A denarius of the reign of Trajan is datable to between the years 112 and 117, one of the time of Hadrian to 118, and a denarius of Nerva (which it is speculated may have come here along with those) to between the years 96 and 98, AD.

Lowe concludes that "the early inhabitants and Roman rulers must have lived on friendly terms", and Mortimer Wheeler suggested in a paper (published in the *Transactions of the Honourable Society of the Cymmrodorion*, 1920-21) that the Romans used the native population as part of a system of defence. We shall consider again this matter of the relation of the forts to the invasion, but intuitively, it seems unlikely that the Romans would voluntarily have condoned Braich y Dinas's continued viability as a defensive site, during their campaign against the natives, or during their subsequent occupation of northern Wales.

Once again we must be struck by how close together the major hillforts are, implying, if they were at any one time in use together, a density of population which we would not have expected. It would be hard to explain any other chronology for their use: if one existed and had fallen vacant, why build another?

It is only three miles from Braich y Dinas to **Caer Lleion** (also known as Caer Seion), on Conwy Mountain. In between, on a headland which forms an offshoot of the same mountain, lies **Allt Wen**. The three-quarters of a mile between the latter two is even harder to explain, but it must be to do with sight-lines and visibility, and so indicative of one feature of the forts which we shall return to in our conclusions. From Conwy Mountain you can see Penmaenmawr, but you cannot quite see Bwrdd Arthur, above Red Wharf Bay. Evidently some cross-checking of views is felt necessary, because you can see Bwrdd Arthur from Allt Wen. From Conwy Mountain you can see Pen y Gaer, up the Conwy Valley, but only just, and more wholly you can see its neighbouring fort Caer Bach. In the other direction you can see Pen Dinas on a cliff of the Great Orme, and also, from one end of the fort, Bryn Euryn above the Mochdre valley – all places which we shall be visiting shortly. This is a pre-view of their layout. From there the line goes on, into the Clwyd area and along the northern coast, perhaps in unbroken sequence into Cheshire and Shropshire; and from Bwrdd Arthur, as we have seen while on Anglesey, a chain of forts runs with mutual visibility to the extremity of Holyhead. Allt Wen has, then, something instructive to tell us about the layout of a possible network.

It is itself of only slight interest, the main feature of it being the sense of exposure and the view. You come up to the summit plateau through the rampart, though it would be easy at this point to fail to notice it. The single wall is most prominent on the northern side, where there is even a hint of a ditch. Allt Wen is a steep climb, but its reward is that of surveying, as if magisterially, the north coast of Wales.

The fort on the summit of Conwy Mountain is tamer in prominence, and much easier to reach. It is of unusual form, consisting of a half-acre enclosure at the western end, built in an unusually strong and well-finished form, and a long outer rampart enclosing the whole of the summit ridge. What is remarkable is that these two elements seem to form separate units: they each have their entrances from outside, these indeed quite close to each other, but there is no entrance communicating between them.

The larger enclosure, a single-walled structure, encircles some ten and a half acres, and so is relatively small in terms of northern Welsh forts. Once again it makes use of natural features, and has no wall on the north side, where the crags are steepest. Its entrance is surrounded by thicker walling, and excavation showed signs (in the form of post-holes, seemingly designed for four large square posts) of a timber bridge over the top. It is approached by a revetted road, and just to the east of it, a hut built into the wall was evidently a guardhouse, revealing more than four hundred slingstones.

Inside the larger enclosure are the remains of some fifty huts, and seven in the smaller one. Though many of these are simply levelled platforms, some show signs of walling. Three huts were excavated in 1951, though with scant results. Slingstones and rubbing stones, together with a saddle quern, indicate the period known as Iron Age B. The absence of Roman relics, and the lack of any rectangular structures (such as were introduced to both Tre'r Ceiri and Braich y Dinas, which it is known were occupied in Roman times) implies a pre-Roman date of occupation. Indeed, the tumbled piles of its evidently one-high masonry leads us to speculate that this was one of the forts which the Romans pulled down.

One thing which the excavators seem certain of is that the forts, both the large and small, belong to two separate periods of development, but not that one succeeded the other: indeed the experts conclude that they were both in use together. The evidence for these points is firstly the fact that a hut lies right across the gateway into the smaller enclosure, which therefore cannot have been the entrance when this fort was first built. The wall of the smaller fort joins that of the larger in such a way as to combine with it to form a face, whereas, if it were replacing it, the route would have simply looped round to continue its circuit.

A feature made much of is usually referred to as the Blocked Entrance, and it lies not in the walls of either fort (as they are in their final form) but in a stretch of outer wall down the slope below the two gateways. This, it is thought, was the line of the original form of the small fort, and the fact that the entrance through it was blocked after a period when it had fallen out of use is revealed by the fact that the north side of it had already collapsed before it was blocked.

This wall outside the entrances (though the blocked entrance within it suggests an earlier use) has a function in relation to the entrance to the small fort which might explain why it was blocked and why the wall was retained. James Dyer, in *Hillforts of England and Wales*, remarks that it was often the custom to stagger the approach, "so that the person entering had to turn to the left for some distance, thus exposing his unshielded sword side to defenders on the rampart above." That would certainly be the effect of this outside stretch of wall, curving below the small fort's major gateway, and with its blocked entrance.

It is this small fort which is best seen today, having been better built in the first place. There are stretches of its facing still visible, and it is possible to trace a well constructed wall-walk. Huts in both cases were built into the ramparts a little to the east of the two entrances in the same style, indicating a contemporary or at least con-cultural design.

The line of the larger one is in some areas difficult to trace. Apart from the north slope, where the wall was never necessary, it in fact runs right round the summit, but on the north-east the wall is ruined and overgrown. The south side is more or less continuous, with signs of facing on the south-west side. Where it meets the south wall of the small fort it swings across the summit to form the small fort's eastern wall. It is here that something surprising occurs. There is a ditch running across the summit alongside the wall at this point, as if to provide defence of the small fort against the interior of the large one. As the Inventory says: "...indeed the small enclosure seems to have been designed to resist attack from the large enclosure as well as from outside." There is, moreover, no entrance-way between the two forts, making the excavators speculate that communication between them would have had to be by ladder. That this would have been located at the north-east corner is indicated by the fact that the ditch system is crossed at that point by a causeway.

The function of this small fort tacked onto the bigger one has been the cause of much discussion. There is nothing quite like it elsewhere in Wales, though something similar apparently happens at Worlebury, in Somerset. The excavators speculated that it might be either a temple or a palace, rejecting the former idea because there is no outstanding hut at its core, and interpreting the palace idea more generally as the enclave of an elite social section. In fact, I think the clue is visible to you as you stand at the edge of this fine defensive position and look down. You see how it commands not only a view of the coast's western approaches, but also of the pass which rises behind it between the hills. But now (and in fact since the Middle Ages) you can see something else of significance. You see the walled town of Conwy with, at one end, its built-on citadel. Conwy castle is a part of the whole complex, yet separate from it and standing independently; indeed, with its drawbridge and portcullis and the narrow and steep approach to it from within the walled town, it is defended not just against the outside world but also against its larger companion. It might seem odd to reason backwards for some 1,300 years, but if we ask ourselves why Conwy takes this form we may get the answer to the same question about Caer Lleion.

The explanation is simple, and indeed in 1646, it was functionally tested: if the town fell, as it did to the Parliamentarians in that August, the castle could still hold, as the Royalist garrison within it proved, for a further three months. The castle was, in other words, an inner citadel, a further line of defence or refuge.

It is too much to suppose that Master James of St. George (the Master of the King's Works in Wales) studied this particular hillfort before designing for Edward this walled town and castle – any more than we need to infer that Edward I himself researched Roman military strategy before deciding to build his fortresses a day's march apart on river entries which could be supplied by sea from Chester, just like the nearby Roman forts. Such apparent coincidences are wonderfully graphic examples of a valuable principle: things take the same form, however elaborate, like the bow and arrow, in diverse and independent communities remote from each other in time and place, because they are human responses to a set of common factors, because they are solutions, moulded by the restrictions of the means at hand, to the same sets of problems.

If Conwy Mountain provides us with an instance of the strongly individual character of our hillforts, so in a different way does **Pen y Gaer**. Here again is a feature unique in England and Wales; but perhaps initially more striking, here once again is a spot most confidently imbued with self-identity.

"It had," says Pennant, writing in the 1770's, "the usual fosses, and vast ramparts of stones, with some remains of the facing of walls, and the foundations of three or four round buildings: but what struck me much, were two considerable spaces of ground thickly set with sharp-pointed stones, set upright in the earth, as if they had been to serve the use of *chevaux de frise*, to impede the approach of an enemy." He goes on to describe the view, wild on the one side rising to the Carneddau, and a bird's-eye-view on the other over the Conwy valley, laid out like a map.

It is probably the view which will strike any one first; the huge uplands stretching towards the mountain wilderness on the one hand, the intricate field-pattern and old land-use on the other, the small farmsteads and winding trackways of the

Tre'r Ceiri

Huts and entrances at Tre'r Ceiri

Mynydd y Twr, Holyhead, where the hillfort overlooks the modern harbour.

Pared Mawr, a little visited area of Llŷn.

Dinas Gynfor, a headland fort overlooking the wild coast of northern Anglesey.

Dinas Gynfor

Dinas Dinlle, a low-lying fort above the beach of a flat coastline.

Yr Eifl from Dinas Dinlle

Porthdinllaen, a simple promortary fort

Garn Fadrun, the central hilltop in Llŷn

Castell Odo, a fully excavated site with a superb outlook

Garn Boduan, site of evidently dense population

Hut on Garn Boduan

An old print showing the large scale settlement at Penmaenmawr

Penmaenmawr headland before quarrying destroyed the hilltop

Pendinas above Llandudno

Mynydd Conwy – the wall of the fort is just visible near the top of the hill.

Caer Bach at Mynydd Conwy – the added citadel

Pen y Gaer, above the Conwy valley

Entrance, Pen-y-Corddyn, not far from Colwyn Bay

Moel Arthur, one of the series of forts along the Clwydian range

Moel y Gaer rises above Dyffryn Clwyd

Moel Fenlli, above Dyffryn Clwyd, with a view from the summit towards the Cheshire Plain

Dinas Brân, above Llangollen

The hilltop of Dinas Brân has been refortified over centuries from Iron Age times.

valley's visible settlement history. But it is the *chevaux de frise* which make Pen y Gaer famous.

It is normally said that the two areas of pointed upright stones in the approaches of Pen y Gaer are the only examples of this form of defence in England and Wales, the other known instances being in the Aran Islands, in Galway Bay off the west coast of Ireland, and in Peebleshire, in the centre of lowland Scotland; places which, on the face of it, could hardly be less connected to each other, or to Pen y Gaer. James Dyer, however, (whose evidence I make much use of), says that another one exists at Craig Gwtheyrn, in Carmarthenshire, and in *Prehistoric Wales* there is said to be another at Caer Euni, in Pembrokeshire – both of which I have yet to see. One area of these still clearly visible stones forms the main approach to the entrance to Pen y Gaer, the other lying on its southern side. The stones probably come from a rock-face on the neighbouring hill of Pen y Gader, where a pile of them may be seen having flaked off the layered cliff.

Hogg, in his *Hill-Forts of Britain*, points to a problem arising from the distribution of *chevaux de frise* in Europe: they are found only in the Iberian Peninsula and in Britain, with no examples in between. Of the three possible explanations, he finds none entirely satisfactory: that the form arose independently in the two areas; that there were in between examples of equivalent structure in wood, which have not been identified; or that small groups of refugees from Spain spread to the unlikely scattered sites in Britain.

A *cheval de frise*, though the form normally occurs in the plural, was originally a portable set of spikes which might be laid to obstruct the passage of cavalry. It was first used, it seems, in the 14th century, and continued to be used by the Austrian infantry against the charges of the Turkish cavalry during the 17th. The term means 'horse of Friesland', a name which it seems to have gained in the Dutch War of Independence from Spain in the mid 16th century, apparently because the Dutch, being short of cavalry, made much use of it to defend breaches in their defences. The name is now applied to the obstacles of spikes or broken glass set on the tops of walls.

The stones which form this remarkable Iron Age defence rise a foot or so above the ground, with a little more below surface. They have a foundation of packed, flat stones, which has kept them in place all these years. There are two groups of them here, one on the western side defending the main entrance, another group to the south where the slope is also easy. Some forty of them can be traced in a 35-square-foot area, standing about a foot apart.

It is perhaps Pen y Gaer's multiple and varied lines of defence which lead the Inventory to proclaim that it is 'almost certainly of several periods', while admitting, however, that no datable evidence has been found. This characteristic is indeed impressive: on the south-west side, for instance, four types of defence are employed, descending the slope. At the top a strong stone wall, still five foot high in places, is fronted by a ledge ahead of the drop to a ditch, which has on the further side a low rampart, then a second ditch, below which a steeper slope falls to a third ditch and a long incline running down to yet a fourth. This determination to defend it is perhaps a sign of Pen y Gaer's importance, and it may be related to its relatively isolated position unusually far inland, its dominance of the river valley, and its proximity to the Roman road rising to cross the hills from Canovium towards Segontium. It is a sign that Pen y Gaer played some crucial role, rather than that it fell and was redesigned (the conventional scenario) by successive invaders.

The finds (after slight excavations carried out in 1905) have been few and disappointing, so do not prove that this hill was permanently populated. There are, however, signs of twelve huts within the inner compound, in the form of level round platforms, and eight more between the inner and the middle walls. Some iron slag which was found indicates the existence of a blast furnace. There are several entrances, though one predominates – a staggered approach from the chevaux de frise in the west, with, inside the outer wall, a modern (perhaps early 19th century) sheepfold set against the Iron Age wall.

Down the slope to the south, a spring breaks, the nearest source of water, and it is in this direction that the ruins of old dwellings may be seen in plentiful numbers, the land above and in the valley of the Afon Dulyn being covered with early field systems and long huts with small enclosures. There are, however, no circular huts, so that it would seem that none of this land use is contemporary with Pen y Gaer, but probably of a late medieval date.

From Pen y Gaer you can see **Caer Bach**, as indeed you can from Conwy Mountain. Caer Bach is once again high up, a round prominence at 1,300 feet on the slopes of Tal-y-fan, and it is indeed small, as its name claims. Once again there are two lines of defence, an outer earthen bank and ditch, and an inner wall of stone. The entrances, on the south-east, have a track approaching them with the characteristic sharp left-turn below the ramparts. One hut within the fort indicates perhaps only temporary occupation. What is remarkable about Caer Bach is the extent of its views to other hillforts, so that we may at least consider this as being connected to its purpose. From it you can see almost in a straight line both Conwy Mountain and Pen Dinas, on the Great Orme.

It has been pointed out to me that **Pen Dinas** (or Pen y Dinas, as it is sometimes known), is the only Iron Age hillfort from which you can see a branch of Woolworths. Certainly the surprise view of the seaside resort of Llandudno spread in all its planned and ordered consistency below is one of the main pleasures of the walk to the edge of this headland. There is not much to be seen of the fort itself. One of its most striking attributes is its central position in relation to other forts. From here one can see both Conwy Mountain and Allt Wen, and even Penmaenmawr. Bryn Euryn is also visible from Pen Dinas, though as we shall shortly see that is a disputed member of this series of Iron Age forts.

Bezant Lowe describes it as an 'excellent example of a Welsh promontory fortress', making the point that, because of the steep cliffs at the end of the spur on which it is set, it was only necessary to defend the neck of the outcrop, the north and north-west side. In his time (1912) there was evidently more to see, and he identifies three lines of defence and the remains of 60-70 huts within an enclosed area of seven acres. The onsite plaque mentions that there were over sixty huts, but the Inventory is of the view that some of the round hollows within the defences were natural. Only five, apparently, are still identifiable. One hut excavated in the mid 19th century revealed animal bones and shellfish and snail shells and a single piece of Samian ware.

The thing that has most interested antiquarians abut Pen Dinas over the centuries is the famous Rocking Stone, Maen Sigl, also known as Cryd Tudno, which lies at one extremity of it, approached by an apparently ancient track. Now it no longer rocks, having been dislodged from its perch in recent times. This is a shame, since the rocking quality was its essential element. "...an immense stone," writes the Rev. Robert Williams, in his 19th century *History of Aberconwy*, "which is so equally poised, that a very slight degree of pressure will enable a person to put it in motion." It was inevitable that folktale would get attached to such a stone, and a local tradition associating it with the Druids is well exemplified in a 1950's booklet, *Llandudno and District in Line and Legend*:

> This is supposed to have been the final arbiter of justice in Druidical times…If, in the trial of one of their subjects no decision as to his guilt or otherwise could be reached, he was led blindfold to the Rocking Stone. If, on touching it, he made it move, he was adjudged innocent. Failure proclaimed his guilt. Punishment was swift death, the unfortunate victim being thrown over the cliff so conveniently near at hand.

It adds, with the usual happy disregard for chronology:

> A numerous community dwelt on this spot in Druidical times. The foundations of a number of round stone huts may still be seen near the Rocking Stone.

Indeed, it seems that there has been in the past more to see at Pen Dinas than there is now. The Rev. Williams says, in 1835, "A wall of great thickness encircles the summit of the hill..." much of which must have been robbed for building purposes later that century. He ascribes the use of the fort, like those on Conwy Mountain and on Penmaenmawr, "not for a constant residence, but only as a place of refuge on the approach of an enemy".

A remarkably fanciful account of the background history of Pen Dinas was written in 1875 by the Rev. Owen Jones, and translated from Welsh by Tom Parry, in 1992. It was, says Jones, perhaps accurately, the refuge to which the natives fled when Agricola's army advanced through North Wales. The Romans then camped where Madoc Street now stands, and they "sent two horsemen to parley with the defenders to surrender" but this "proved fruitless and the Britons refused to relinquish their fortress". The Romans moved a section of their army to attack Pen Dinas from the rear "but many of the gallant defenders realised this, set fire to the camp and attacked the encamped troops when many of them were killed in the engagement...As a result of this the Romans over-ran the fortress and mercilessly slew those within, causing the natives to call it, 'Creuddin' or, 'The Bloody Fort' ". The Rev. Jones does not explain how he knows so much detail of an event which is nowhere else recorded.

Located at such a pivotal position between the two angles of coast, neatly linking the end of one of them, Pen Dinas, with the succession of others reaching towards Clwyd, **Bryn Euryn** should, in all reasonableness, be an Iron Age fort. It has the air of one, the height and the exposure, and the view to others of the same nature, not just Pen Dinas, but Conwy Mountain, Penmaenmawr, Pen y Gaer and Caer Bach all being visible from this focal central lookout. Being in such elevated spots is very much (we can see) an Iron Age habit. But Bryn Euryn is thought to be a Dark Age site, and indeed, elsewhere such Dark Age defences as Dinas Emrys and Deganwy do make use as well of height and exposure. The fort here has been partially excavated, in 1997, but no evidence was found which would date it. There were some characteristics which were not felt to be typical of Iron Age work, and in fact more characteristic of the Dark Age and early medieval periods. That is, (records the Preliminary Report), it consists of a small citadel with outworks, and 'does not have the characteristic bank and ditch construction of a typical Iron Age fort'. The report notes, though, that within the outer rampart or enclosure are the remains of a possible round house of Iron Age or Roman British date, and another lies not far off in the wood known as Coed y Gaer. Whatever lack of evidence there is for either dating, we cannot rule out a prior use by the people of our period, any more than we can imagine them resisting such a prime location.

There is not much to be seen of the fort, whatever age it was, on Bryn Euryn now. A limestone bank is clear in places, and there are some traces of stone facing. Increasingly, the spread of blackthorn obscures any further work on the north-west and north-east sides.

THE EASTERN GROUP

Above Llanddulas, perched on a limestone escarpment above the steep valley of the river Dulas, about a mile and a quarter from the sea, just behind the little village of Rhyd y Foel, sprawls the massive enclosure of **Pen y Corddyn**, often known quite justifiably as Pen y Corddyn Mawr. Estimates vary as to how many acres are enclosed, but it seems to be in the area of the high thirties. The site was excavated by Dr. Willoughby Gardner in 1905, revealing that the walls of well-constructed masonry appeared to have been deliberately thrown down. Only one piece of pottery was found, and no trace of permanent dwellings; but any conclusions this might lead us to are confounded by the discovery of refuse tips containing broken animal bones, pot-boilers and charcoal indicating cooking – all evidence of occupation – which the character of the pottery suggests as the early centuries AD. Sling stones suggest at least a garrison use, but the large extent of the enclosed area would surely indicate use as at least a refuge for a much larger number of people and their stock.

High on its limestone crag, Pen y Corddyn has a view to the sea, and in the eastern direction, the next hillfort, **Castell Cawr** (now much wooded and hard to see), and probably several beyond it, is encompassed by its panorama. On the inland side, what it particularly has to offer is the unspoilt view of rolling farmland, textured with its old field patterns and seamed by winding lanes hidden in high hedges and by hedgerow trees, a curiously wide view of a villageless world, its township composed of the evenly-spaced substantial farms which are its main landmarks. A great and timeless peace pervades this land, all sounds distanced beyond earshot, except the occasional and somehow comforting agricultural ones. On this inner side, the world is enclosed by its own encircling ridge. By contrast to seaward, to the north-east, there is a distant view of Rhyl, and indeed on a clear day, of Liverpool.

The main feature of Pen y Corddyn now is its main entrance, still impressive, of which Christopher Hawkes says in his comprehensive paper 'Hill-Forts' in the March 1931 edition of *Antiquity:* "The northeast Y-Cordynn entrance (*sic*) is an extreme development of the old inturned type, with rectangular guard-house bays which, while they suggest imitation of a Roman gate-plan, recall the guard-house of St. Catherine's Hill and Leckhampton." He cites Willoughby Gardner and Mortimer Wheeler in this connection in support of the theory, which we have already encountered, that Roman influence was a result of the occupants of the hillforts being used as a sort of mercenary force by the Romans, defending the coast against invaders, though one wonders whether they could do this effectively after their defensive walls were pulled down.

If Dr. Gardner had little luck at Pen y Corddyn, he and his successor Dr. H.N. Savory made up for this in their extensive excavations of nearby **Dinorben**, which tells us much of what we know about the use and occupation of Iron Age hillforts in Britain.

It is ironic that we now find, not for the first time and not quite the last, that the forts we know the most about are those which are no longer there. A vast hole in the earth now represents the place on which the great fort of Dinorben stood. It was Dinorben's misfortune to have been built on fine white limestone, the demand for which increased with its use in industry, notably in the great steel-works such as those at Shotton. (The role of lime in the production of iron and steel lies in its ability to remove impurities). There was a quarry here already by 1912; by the 1940's it was encroaching on the fort's northern defences.

Also known as Parc y Meirch, the former hilltop on which the fort once stood lies above the present settlement of St. George. This is something of a mistranslation, since the Welsh saint, Sant Sior, is not the same personage as the patron saint of England, but was, in lore, connected with horses. Hence the alternative name of the fort. A holy well apparently lay (perhaps still lies, in a ruined form, inside the gates of Kinmel Park) at the place now called St. George, to which sick horses were brought to be cured. However, the fort and other features in the area, such as a manor house and a farm, bore the name Dinorben (in its earlier form, Dynorben Vaur) since at least as early as the 14th century. The 'din' is of course a fort, and Orben perhaps a personal name. Pennant refers to it as Pen y Parc, "a very strong post", and repeats an evidently local tale that it was occupied by Owain Gwynedd, in a stand-off before the army of Henry II. If indeed that took place here, after the battle at Basingwerk, then the site was in use for at least 1400 years. More, perhaps, since Fenton in 1808 mentions a 'modern' beacon, which cannot (as is sometimes thought) have been part of the celebrations (like the tower on Moel Famau) of the Jubilee of the reign of George III, since that did not take place until 1810.

The area had come to the attention of antiquarians in 1868 with the discovery of a Bronze Age bronze horse harness at the foot of the crags, the only indication, however, that the place has a Late Bronze Age connection.

Professional investigation of the fort on Dinorben hill started with a 'Perambulation' of the site by Dr. Willoughby Gardner in 1911, to see what was left of it, by then overgrown with trees. Dr. Gardner had already had experience of hillforts from a dig at Pen y Gaer in 1905 and the one already referred to on Pen y

Corddyn in the same year. He noted initially that at two places the main rampart had been thrown down, "completely covering the middle rampart" for a stretch, indicating that the fort had been taken and disarmed.

Dr. Gardner led excavations in 1912, 1913 and 1914. There was then a break for the War, but he was back in November 1919, and the last phase of this series of excavations took place in the spring of 1922. The fort was then neglected because it was expected to be totally destroyed, but what was then left of it was further investigated, now under Dr. Savory, starting in October 1956 and continuing in 1957, '58, '59 and 1961.

The fort was not large, being about five acres, compared to Pen y Corddyn's thirty-seven and the Clwydian forts of Pen y Cloddiau, at some fifty acres, and Foel Fenlli at twenty-five. It is the wealth of discovery and the fortunate rare datability of it which marks it out as special.

The excavators (as later at Castell Odo on Llŷn) came to some fairly confident conclusions. They saw the site as having been occupied in distinct phases, with gaps between them. An open village preceded the first fortifications, lasting from 300 to 200 BC. Then, five acres were enclosed by a rampart and ditch, though the lack of pottery finds might indicate a cattle enclosure rather than a populated site. When pottery is scarce elsewhere, however, this does not always mean the place was uninhabited, since as we have seen, the so-called 'Highland Zone' native culture managed without pottery, an innovation brought to the area by southern immigrants. This fortified (or at least enclosed) location was in any case apparently destroyed by fire, indicating perhaps an invasion.

We then enter the Roman period. Some 2nd century pottery and metalwork is found, particularly an ox-head ornament, known as an escutcheon, which may have been worn suspended as an amulet. The report concludes that this late phase of re-use was "connected with British resistance to the advance of Rome" and that it ended "with the partial demolition of the defences, presumably at the hands of the Romans, and the abandonment of the site by its inhabitants."

The fort was then unused for a long period. When it was re-occupied it was no longer fortified. That was in late Roman times, AD 260 to 355. Coins now make dating easier and more certain. The archaeologists see this re-occupation as a reflection of the insecurity which came with the gradual withdrawal of the legions. "It is likely that this reoccupation of a half-demolished hill-fort reflects the effect upon the civil population of north-east Wales of insecurity at a time when the Irish were frequently raiding and even settling on the west coasts of Britain, and the small Roman garrisons which were still maintained...were not always able to come to the assistance of the provincials quickly." But then, we wonder, why did they not rebuild the defences?

Dr. Gardner found the entrance, which had been deliberately blocked, with several layers of roadway running through it, successively covered over and rebuilt. There were post-holes indicating a gate, and the fact that some had charcoal at the bottom indicated that when the entrance was first destroyed, the woodwork had been consumed by fire.

We shall be looking at the finds from Dinorben in more detail in the next chapter, because they are practically all we have to go on to identify the dates and use of the hillforts, and the way of life of the people who built them. It was a surprise to Dr. Gardner to find that, although there is ample sign of habitation, the huts of Dinorben did not have stone foundations, providing those visible rings so characteristic of the period, but evidently lay on levelled round platforms or hollows, and being made of wood, or rather wattle and daub, left no remains other than patches of burnt clay. Only detailed investigation would have found them, so that once again we have to qualify our assertions. When it is said that a hillfort contains no huts, or few, we should perhaps rather say that none or few have been found. Though they ate the same shell-fish here as at Penmaenmawr, a wider meat diet was evident, consisting of domesticated rather than hunted animals, and, unusually, horses. Fragments of food and cooking jars and grinding bowls were found, the usual paraphernalia of cooking and eating which seem, everywhere, to get broken and left. Some pieces of the superior Samian ware, imported from Gaul, give witness (as at Penmaenmawr) to an element of luxury. Dr. Gardner (in his summary of the digs in *The Heart of Northern Wales*) gives the opinion that, with the exception of a few bits of coarse pottery which were perhaps made on the spot, most of what was found at Dinorben was of Romano-British origin, "brought into the district by traders from the large Romano-British towns in the midlands." He notes that the items were valued by their owners: they had frequently been mended with rivets, whereas in the towns where such things came from, riveted specimens were rare.

The fact that the inhabitants used saddle querns rather than rotary querns for grinding their corn indicates that they were not much exposed to Roman influence. We make our inferences of course from what remains, since anything destructible had gone. Stone spindle whorls indicate wooden spindles. Stone pot-boilers imply a skin-lined cooking hole. Iron corrodes when exposed, and much iron-work has probably disintegrated. There were arrow and spear heads, and a large number of sling stones, clearly the favoured weapon of the time. Of the first three of the four phases of fortification which he identifies, Dr. Gardner says that as at nearby Pen y Corddyn, the forts were occupied for short periods only, "as shown by the small amount of silting found in the ditches and the paucity of relics left behind by the occupiers." In the last phase, by contrast, a large number of people lived there continuously for some time, until their fort was destroyed towards the end of the fourth century, after which they never came back.

The remarkable band of limestone which runs through northern Wales from eastern Anglesey in an arc which ends in the Vale of Llangollen, skirts the coast east of Dinorben, and outcrops above Dyserth, near Rhuddlan, where the next in this chain of hillforts, **Moel Hiraddug**, has also suffered from the hunger of industry for lime. The encroachment of Dyserth limestone quarry led to rescue operations being carried out in the form of excavations under the auspices of the Ministry of Works, in 1954 and 1955. The results are recorded by the director of the work, Christopher Houlder, under the title *Rescue Excavations at Moel Hiraddug*, published by the Flintshire Historical Society in 1961.

The northern part of the fort was threatened, about a third of the whole, and it was there Houlder concentrated his investigation. The fort lies on the northern end of a limestone escarpment, rising to 867 feet, and in this case even the steep side is defended, but with only one stone rampart. On the eastern side, where the slope is less severe, there are three lines of defence. The outer rampart consists of a bank, with some facing stone, and a ditch; the middle one is of stone, though poorly preserved, with no ditch; the innermost line runs on top of the scarp, accompanied by a ditch, and is the best preserved. It is 16 foot thick, and faced.

As elsewhere the gates are of interest. That at the north-west was originally twelve foot wide with turned-in ramparts embracing it, and a guard-hut alongside. The approach to the inner main gateway can be seen to run below the rampart for 200 feet.

Few huts were found, but some hollows possibly indicate the whereabouts of more, and the usual stores of slingstones link this fort with many others. Such scant pieces of pottery as were found could not be dated. The evidence, Houlder says, was too scanty "to evaluate the known periods of the history of the fort in cultural terms". One hut which was excavated yielded a jet toggle. Houlder sees the ramparts as being chronologically successive, and found evidence of the fort having been attacked and reoccupied. He draws from this a number of conclusions, which we must regard as hypothetical: "now the absolute date of the event" – the fort's destruction – "can be defined within certain limits, and the fall of the hillfort for which the middle rampart provided the main defence on the east can be put, with reserve, within a few years after the start of the first century A.D." The evidence of the '54-'55 excavations, he says, leads to the conclusion that the history of Moel Hiraddug "must have been comparatively short, spanning perhaps two centuries in all." The lack of hard evidence does not stop him elaborating on the background situation: "...the mere fact of the capture and refortification of the site at this late date, arguably by a newly arrived group of people under pressure from the east, must indicate a major event in the tribal history of North Wales." Yet, without further proof it is not really a 'fact'; the attackers might as well have been local; and if they did come from elsewhere it could just as well have been from the west.

Just as at Dinorben, the most interesting find (there the discovery of a bronze horse harness) had happened in 1868, long before the professionals got there, so at Moel Hiraddug, the finding of fragments of a shield of La Tène style – that is, the second phase of the Iron Age – datable to about the second century BC, took place in 1872. The find consisted of parts of a number of curved plates, together with two pieces of an iron sword blade. These lay under about three feet of rubble from a collapsed rampart, and since it is agreed that this would be an unlikely place to bury them for ceremonial purposes, it is assumed that the collapse of the wall and the loss of the valuable objects were related to the same event. Nothing more of this sort, unfortunately, has been found.

Moel Hiraddug today reveals none of this. It is a prominent landmark overlooking the broad and level Clwyd plain, its summit ridge looking out towards the long flat coast between Rhyl and Prestatyn, with the valley of the Clwyd stretching to its south-west, and rolling farmland cutting off the horizon to the east. You can see on this side the treble banks of its defences, largely levelled now, with a line of stones on top in places, and below the top on what looks like natural scree, which may, at one time, have been piled up into a wall. The quarry abruptly cuts off its northern end, and the long limestone ridge becomes a vast gaping hole. Across the wide valley, at the far side of the silt plain of the Clwyd, the fort at Dinorben, when it was still there, would have been visible from here.

As we move along the rim of the Clwyd valley, the forts confront us even more than elsewhere with the problem of their number and their proximity. It has been speculated that they formed some sort of boundary, perhaps between the uplands and the lowlands. W. E. Griffiths, for instance, who was Principal Investigator for the Royal Commission, writes in Dodd's *A History of Wrexham:* "So it may be that in pre-Roman times a conscious frontier was being developed between the hill folk and the men of the lowlands." Certainly it is more credible to see them as collaborative rather than competitive. To have so much assertive rivalry within so small a range is not compatible with the context of organised agriculture in which we know they were set. Nor is it likely that they were chronologically successive, since, if such a fort had fallen out of use, the natural thing would be to rebuild it rather than to build another one nearby. It is further speculated, however, that they may not all be pre-Roman: Sir Cyril Fox found that the line of Offa's Dyke, in the neighbourhood of the hillfort at Y Gardden, might have been influenced by the fact that the latter was occupied by the Welsh at the time of its construction, about AD 790. Yet its occupation then could of course be a re-use, and does not disqualify it from construction in pre-Roman times.

Pen y Cloddiau lies between Nannerch and Llandyrnog, in (or rather above) an area of forestry. It sprawls across its hilltop providing breathtaking and widely extensive views ranging from the upper reaches of the Vale of Clwyd spread out like a level sheet between its rolling hills, to the sea – at the coast beyond Glanwydden; and from the summit another wide view north to Merseyside, over the Wirral to Liverpool and Birkenhead.

Pen y Cloddiau is on the Offa's Dyke long-distance footpath, and so quite well known. It is said to be the largest hillfort in Wales, its double bank and ditch enclosing some 52 acres.

If part of the purpose was all-round vision, the success in this respect of building on Pen y Cloddiau surely made **Moel Arthur**, less than a mile and a half away, redundant from the start. Steep-sided and round, rising to about 1,500 feet, it has substantially the same views as its greater neighbour. Maybe what it has in addition is the advantage (lacked by Pen y Cloddiau) of looking towards Moel Famau, the highest point of the Clwydian Range. Yet there is no evidence that Moel Famau (likely as it seems) was the site of a hillfort; and Moel Fenlli, the other side, is masked from Moel Arthur.

Moel Fenlli itself forms a sort of end to our chain of Clwydian forts, looking out as it does onto different country. If you come up from the lane out of Llanbedr Dyffryn Clwyd, you will be impressed by its natural defences of elevation and steep slopes. It is surprising that it was considered necessary to defend this side at all, but it bears towards the top a double earthen bank. There is, however, an easier route to it by a footpath from the top of the pass, and whichever way you come, you are about to be surprised. Foel Fenlli owes its air of definitive status to the fact that it looks both ways. Coming up from the south-west you turn to see the whole stretch of the Vale of Clwyd. From the round top of this 1,500 foot hill, when you reach it, a view stretches the other way into England, far away to that other fertile farmland, the distant spread of the Cheshire plain.

There are many lesser forts in this evidently densely populated area, in Iron Age times, two of them confusingly called **Moel y Gaer**. The eastern of these looks towards the Dee coast near Flint, and the western one near Pistyll, just north of Bodfari, springs a further surprise by having extensive views to the north-east all the way to the sea at Penrhyn Bay, so that this deeply rural outpost (consisting of some outer quite weak ramparts with double banks on the summit, separated from each other by a steep v-shaped ditch) turns out to be a coastal look-out eight miles from the nearest sea. At the eastern Moel y Gaer, the one between Rhosesmor and Halkyn, some excavation has been done. A Bronze Age palisade was found to predate the main rampart, and round huts inside the enclosure were also thought to be possibly Bronze Age. The fort fell out of use from a period as early as the fifth century B.C. (one hut produced evidence of occupation until about 820 B.C., and others until about 350), and was possibly re-occupied in about 370 B.C., being then given a new rampart. It was, therefore, very old when it was finally abandoned during the Roman period.

A great stream of these forts stretches southwards, and out of our area – though we cannot help feeling that they are relevant to our understanding of the northern-Wales hillforts' nature, and so a small selection of them will be briefly mentioned here.

Some of these, like a few we have considered, show signs of successive use. A prime example is **Dinas Brân**, above Llangollen, where the romantic medieval ruin is surrounded by an encircling bank and ditch of Iron Age times, and Iron Age hut floors have been found within the medieval fort. Also in the border area, lies one of the most impressive Iron Age forts in Britain, the massive bulk of **Old Oswestry**, which, we feel, must have been a major tribal centre. Here, a remarkable series of five ditches and banks defends the westerly approach, seven in fact around the west gate itself, indicating that the fort was designed to protect the fertile land to the east from attack from the direction of what is now Wales. Surprisingly, little in the way of evidence of habitation has been recovered from the wide flat area within the ramparts, though some Bronze Age material found there indicates a long period of use.

Though Old Oswestry is low-lying in location, others in the border area are notably prominent. The **Breiddin** is on a cliff at the edge of an escarpment, perched over the valley at Criggion (the subject of a thorough excavation by C. R. Musson, published in 1991, which, unfortunately, cannot be dealt with here), and perhaps more famously **the Wrekin**, on its rhyolitic crag, hardly needed to be defended at all, so sheer is the slope on most of its sides. This, for once, has been shown to have been most probably a permanently occupied site, belonging to two closely successive periods of use. It appears to have been burnt, perhaps in the fifth century BC, and then rebuilt further up the slope. A general lack of Romano-British finds indicates that it fell out of use at the time of the conquest, and perhaps, by no coincidence, there appears to have been a second fire about AD 50, when the Roman troops were already in the valley below. At the Breiddin, on the other hand, finds of some Roman pottery show that use went on, although here, once again, such use also started early. This clifftop, overlooking a bend in the meandering Severn, was in use as early as 1000 BC; its first palisade, with posts a metre apart, being dated at 975 and lying, significantly, under a later stone rampart. All this is by now a familiar pattern: the wooden palisade structure pre-dating the stone-built one, the alternative of apparent destruction at a certain date in Roman times or of continued use witnessed by Roman finds.

There are two forts called **Caer Caradoc**, supposed sites of the last stand of the famous Roman-period king, one near Knighton, just south of the river Clun; the other further north and nearer to Wroxeter, at Church Stretton. This remarkable volcanic cone is of interest since it appears to have been a permanent settlement, judging by the number of huts within its exposed and constricted compound. At 1,500 feet above the Church Stretton valley (the only pass through this generally rugged area), through the constriction of which the Roman road ran to Viroconium, it is so steep and so windy a spot that one wonders, even while savouring the extensive sight of the folded ridges lying above the Shropshire plain, what demands can have led to so extreme a form of defiance and determination. Caer Caradoc gives the feeling of being at the edge of something, and its location in geography, at the interface of the first settled Roman area and the heartland of northern Wales, gives it a pivotal position in history too.

THREE

IRON AGE TIMES

Iron had been in use for some time in the Middle East before it arrived in Britain, during the first thousand years or so B.C. Its use in Europe is associated with movement, the migration of people perhaps owing something to the increased efficiency which came with the new metal, although already in the later Bronze Age a settled pattern of farming had produced circumstances of agricultural surplus (as evidenced by the specialisation and available time needed to build great monuments) which, in turn, would give rise to an expanding population and an increasing competition for fertile land.

We cannot, in fact, too rigorously distinguish the two periods, and the discovery of later Bronze Age ceramics in embryo hillforts (such as at Castell Odo), means that we should not see this new form as having been brought to Britain along with other Iron Age things by a wave of invaders. There was some shift, however, as a recognisable new form of society developed: we later see continental influence occurring, as if the populations of Britain and mainland Europe were connected, and kept in touch.

The idea of carving the past up in such a way that we might talk of an 'Iron Age' occurred first in a book by C. J. Thomsen in 1836, and its connection with people who came to be known as 'the Celts' was largely due to discoveries made at Hallstatt, a village in Austria, by an archaeologist called G. Ramsauer between 1846 and 1862, and further by discoveries at La Tène, at the east end of Lake Neuchatel in Switzerland in 1858. The styles of the artefacts at these two sites were recognisably different to what had been found elsewhere, and sufficiently distinct from each other to give two type groups, which came to be seen as representing an earlier and a later development of the culture of the Iron Age, or Celtic, people. As to whether 'Celtic' is the right term, all I can do here (since this technicality is definitely a different subject) is to issue a word of caution. The word refers to a language-group within the Indo-European family of languages, and we do not know what tongue these pre-literate people spoke. The term Celtic has been widely adopted, by extension, to refer to the cultural style of the presumed ancestors of the Celtic-speaking people, precisely these Iron Age base populations of the Hallstatt and La Tène cultural groups.

The whole business of classifying Iron Age people and activity in Britain owes much to the work of Christopher Hawkes, whose paper in the March 1931 edition of *Antiquity* entitled 'Hill-Forts, A Retrospect', has been of seminal importance to academic thinking on the subject. Hawkes saw the Early Iron Age as stemming from the sixth century B.C. (though modern dating, now having the advantage of radiocarbon analysis, would make it earlier). He speculated that the causes of the building of the earlier forts must have been either the circumstance of a constant threat of warfare, or tribal hostilities arising from population growth. The Hallstatt influence in Britain came with a growth in commerce and in craftsmanship, with increased contact with the Mediterranean, where such fortifications were already established. The transition from bronze to iron, as Hawkes sees it, led to a spreading west of refugees.

At this time, Germanic people were pressing from the Baltic south and putting pressure on the Celts of the lower Rhine, from the 7th century BC. This led to 'Late Hallstatt immigrant groups' in Britain and, in turn, to a change in life-style and thus, in due course, to the hillforts. Hawkes sees the hillforts as "citadels of tribal groups". By the end of the 6th century BC, the Celts of northern Spain became linked to the south-west of Britain by the Atlantic tin trade. Here, we come to the arrival of La Tène type material, and to Iron Age B, characterised by close links with Brittany. This second phase was characterised (in the Hawkes model) by larger and more elaborate hillforts. This scheme of Hawkes's would not now be universally accepted without further qualification, but it has served well enough as a rough tool. Sir Mortimer Wheeler wrote, for instance (in 1939): "In 1931 Mr. C. F. C. Hawkes...introduced a welcome measure of order to this medley of British Iron Age cultures by grouping them into three main categories: A, B and C." 'C' will not concern us here, being confined to the south and south-east, but for the record it consists of the two 'Belgic' invasions, the first from northern Gaul into Kent around 75 B.C., the second after Caesar's conquest of Gaul, refugees pushing west into Hampshire and West Sussex (meeting some Iron Age A resistance, evidenced by refortification) just before the Roman invasion.

Some, or all, of these are related to the people Caesar observed in Gaul, of whom he remarked that not only every tribe, but almost every family, is divided into rival factions. He saw their society as being highly hierarchical, and dominated by the priesthood, the Druids. When he came to Britain he found a dense population, living in houses similar to those of the Gauls, and herding cattle. He describes an assault on a British 'stronghold', which he defines as a densely wooded spot (surprisingly) 'fortified with a rampart and trench, to which they retire in order to escape the attacks of invaders.' He makes it clear that they took their cattle in to it with them.

What we know about the way of life of these people largely concerns these various points touched on by Caesar: they farmed (not just cattle, since field-systems are associated with their dwellings); they took part in warfare; and the number of their 'strongholds' indicates that they had need of defence, either, through being divided into rival factions, from each other, or from a common enemy, such as him.

A.H.A. Hogg (he who undertook the 1950's excavations at Garn Boduan and Tre'r Ceiri), wrote an important book *Hill-Forts of Britain* in the 1970's, which updates some of the conclusions arrived at by Hawkes by seeing a greater continuity in the earlier hillforts from British Late Bronze Age times, the continental influences arriving later. He says that the nature of the pottery "suggests that the population consisted mostly of the people who lived in Britain during the Late Bronze Age – a view confirmed by the survival of round houses as the predominant type, in contrast to the frequency of rectangular buildings on the continent". It is with Iron Age B that a wave of foreign influences arrived in Britain, about 300 to 250 BC, when the 'A' culture had only just begun to replace the Late Bronze Age in the north and west. Hogg is interesting about the provenance of this pottery. We think of these people as being busy making these pots themselves, but evidently specialisation had begun by then, and they had other things to do. "Much, if not all, of this pottery " (Hogg informs us) " was produced commercially in particular districts, and distributed by trade." He cites and qualifies Caesar: his evidence suggests "a society dominated by Priests (Druids) and warriors" but "the great mass of people were essentially farmers". Farming in the south and east and the Welsh Marches was primarily arable, but cattle predominated in Wales.

Hogg has shown, and others agree, that the first forts were made with simple palisades, which were shortly replaced with single ramparts. It is generally thought that the introduction of multiple ramparts was a product of a second wave of defensive building, in one set of theories being the reworking of a conquered fort by the invaders who had taken it. The Ancient Monuments Inventory for our area, for instance, says "It seems a reasonable inference that the Bivallate Forts represent the occupation of the earlier sites by invaders", from the sea, we may suppose, since most of them here lie within three miles of the northern Welsh coast.

Hogg estimates the population at the time as being of the same density as in the 12th century AD: four to six people per square kilometre in Wales (though I suppose in concentrated clusters, in an empty land). "In modern Britain population as sparse as this is only found near the remoter mountain districts." They died young. The evidence of the cemeteries at Maiden Castle is that out of 39 bodies 11 died in infancy; 19 below 40; 4 between 40 and 50, and one, the oldest, between 45 and 55. Forty years was therefore "the longest term one could reasonably hope for, even if one survived the dangers of childhood".

It is the new arrivals who are credited with the introduction of the sling as a weapon, and it was this, it is reasonable to suppose, which led to the invention, perhaps originating in Britain, of defences consisting of two or three or more close-set banks and ditches.

The principle is basic: when people are going to fight you hand to hand you want them up fairly close, but with yourself on top behind a rampart, so that you can drop things on them or hit them on the head. When both sides are fighting with slings you want to keep them out of reach of firing at you but in such a position that you are able to fire at them. The sling stone goes further, one must suppose, downhill, than up. Hence, at this point, the vertical upper rampart (which would in fact provide cover from sling fire if it were reached, when it could then be undermined) is now supported by a bank and a wide ditch, both of which have to be crossed unprotected, and the bank (noticeably) slopes outwards, so that there is no dead ground on its outer side. A steeper face on its inner side prevents retreat. The strategy of defensive construction has in effect been reversed.

Thus, Sir Mortimer Wheeler, for instance, reporting in 1939 on his excavations of Maiden Castle, comments that a single line of defence was extended suddenly in the first century BC to several; "methods of defence are conditioned by methods of attack". The use of slings is attested by the finds of very numerous rounded beach pebbles. The same have been found in several of our northern Wales sites, such as at Garn Boduan and Conwy Mountain.

A further conclusion is suggested by Hogg to arise from these new conditions, which is certainly worth considering, though work would have to be done to prove it: the apparent duplication of forts in some areas is due to an earlier fort not being convertible, for reasons of terrain, to the new conditions of sling warfare, so being more easily replaced on more suitable ground for this new purpose with a new design.

Why, we may well wonder, did the sling take so long to be reinvented, since one thing we know for certain about it is that it was around in Biblical times? Sling stones have also been found in connection with Bronze Age sites in Greece (for instance in fortifications dating from the 3rd to the first part of the 2nd millennium BC on the island of Skyros), so that it is puzzling to find that it seems to have fallen out of use for so long. In any case, we should note (when we come to consider the hillforts' use in the next, concluding chapter) that there is plenty of evidence of violence here, even before the Roman assaults: the sling-stone dumps of many excavations show preparations for defence; burnt gateways and burnt rampart timbering show factual evidence of actual attack.

Archaeologists give us no reason to think that such events as these were either universal or frequent. Indeed, the very strength of the hillforts would, in general, have deterred assault. When such events happened in the context of Romano-British finds at the end of the fort's main period of use, it is easy to see them as the imposition of *pax Romana* on an ungrateful nation, and to put an approximate date on them accordingly. It is when they occur much earlier (as at Castell Odo) that they need to be explained. We have to ask then: who was fighting whom? It is natural to see this as part of a competition for viable land. Occupation of the local hillfort, one may suppose, was a prerequisite of control over that land. Those who got there first – the pattern is familiar – defended their acquired interests against intrusion by people arriving later. The proximity of many forts to the coastline makes us guess that the newcomers arrived by sea or up river valleys, probably, therefore, from the European continent, and we know that right at the end of the hillforts' active period, raiders came in large numbers from what is now Ireland to a country now no longer defended by the Romans.

For what these people looked like, we have to rely once again on the Roman historians. It is Caesar himself who says that the Britons all dyed their bodies with woad, which was blue, though whether they did this all the time or only to give themselves "a more terrifying appearance in battle" is not quite clear. They had long hair, and shaved the whole of the rest of their bodies except their moustaches. It is Tacitus (in *Agricola*) who says, rather surprisingly, that the Britons were of several ethnic types – in which we may see the basis of Hawkes's several waves of immigrants, A, B and C. "Physical characteristics," Tacitus says, "vary, and that very variation is suggestive." In Scotland they are reddish haired and large limbed, which he takes to be a Germanic type; in what is now southern Wales they are dark and curly-haired, which Tacitus sees as influence from Spain; on the south coast they are just like the Gauls, and have the same rituals and beliefs, and "there is no great difference in language".

If Tacitus is at all accurate – and the rest of his description of Britain would lead us to think he was well-informed – then he provides a useful correction to the simplistic view of a Celtic Britain of pre-Roman times. It was already a diverse population.

Although the Romans tell us this was a highly stratified society, the archaeologists are unable to corroborate this. Hogg notes the apparent egalitarian character of the hilltop villages. It is, he says, rarely that one can identify any dwelling significantly larger than the others, which might have been the house of a chief. At least, he qualifies this, such places have not yet been found.

That these people were tribally organised is also attested by the Roman authors, but as a result we have for these tribes only Romanised names. In our area of present concern there were in all four tribes, and the similarity of their artefacts, such indeed as their hillforts, must lead us to suppose that they did not regard themselves as culturally distinct, in fact, that they shared ideas and a way of life. On the Llŷn peninsula and along the Menai Strait and the north coast as far as the Conwy valley lived a tribe known as the Gangani, (a name mentioned in this connection by the 2nd century Greek geographer Ptolemy), which Cunliffe (in *Iron Age Communities in Britain*) says were "presumably related to a tribe of the same name living in north-west Ireland". In other words Llŷn was, as one might expect, an Irish colony, as was probably Anglesey as well. According to other authorities this tribe was known as the Venedotae, a name which later gave to the area the term Gwynedd. East of the Conwy valley lay the Deceangli, who spread as far as the river Dee and south into the Clwyd valley. There, they bordered with the Cornovii, whose territory ran from Chester to Shrewsbury.

South of the Vendotae and the Deceangli lay the lands of the Ordovices, in the Snowdonia mountains and running southwards to mid-Wales.

The pattern of the movement of hillfort development into Wales, at least as far as can be traced from the available evidence, followed the same form as that for Britain as a whole. The earliest sites have Late Bronze Age roots, as has been shown at Dinorben. The first walls built were probably more cattle compounds than defensive sites: Hogg points out that all that would be needed to move from field boundaries to ramparts is "some stimulus which would make the work worthwhile", such as might come with an increase in population in conditions of settled farming. His useful book gives us much detail of the technical side of hillfort-building, and the construction of the huts within them. A workforce of 200 people (assuming 150 men, with women and children carrying baskets) could build a fort of 3.4 hectares (these calculations being based on work done at Ladle Hill, in Hampshsire) in 85 to 115 days. In his report on Garn Boduan and Tre'r Ceiri, he gave his estimate of the density of population, based on occupancy of five people per hut, as between 13 and 21 persons per acre, that is, presumably, within the hillforts. This, he points out, shows a remarkable consistency over time: the population for Conwy in 1305 had a density of 24 persons per acre. Assuming further that the occupants of each hut took part in building the ramparts, contributing five cubic yards a day, the building of the second phase at Garn Boduan would take 67 days, the first phase of Tre'r Ceiri 78.

Hogg contributes much to our knowledge of the detailed construction of the huts, but first, he has a valuable correction to make to our way of thinking of them in general. Though we demean them with the term 'huts', 'hut circles', he points out that they are better thought of as houses – a round dwelling of seven metre diameter is equivalent in square footage to the footprint of a modern two-bedroomed bungalow; and less than 10 metres of circular diameter covers the same ground as a three-bedroomed bungalow with two reception rooms. The 'huts' are usually between 6 and 8 metres in diameter, and can be up to 15.

Examples excavated at Tre'r Ceiri and elsewhere have shown that these dwellings were divided into rooms, separated probably by hangings or boarded partitions, with a central living space and a hearth near the middle. The walls are 1.5 metres high at most, usually less than one metre, so that as the conical roof appears to have rested on the top of the wall itself, the edges of the interior space would be low, and therefore used for sleeping. The pitch of the roof was determined by the mechanics of construction over so large a diameter, but there are signs that it was further supported, in some cases, by posts set inside the circle. In such dwellings elsewhere, the smoke from the hearth is simply allowed to dissipate naturally through the thatch, so that, for instance, in the villages of the hill tribes of Thailand, the whole village appears to be on fire.

The walls are universally dry-stone: there was no use of mortar. Hogg tells us that the quality of workmanship both of walling and carpentry was up to the standard of the Middle Ages. One problem for him is that, though most of the buildings were round, following the British tradition derived from the Bronze Age, there were some that were square. "The problem of the relationship between round and rectangular houses has not yet been solved." A simple supposition would be, of course, that the squarer ones were later, following the imported Roman style or influenced by its adoption in continental Europe. If the time-sequence does not fit, it could further be supposed that the round style was reintroduced in a renaissance of earlier tradition.

Many of the forts have, in addition to interior buildings, a series of pits, which it is thought were for storing grain, and when they became stale from this were used as depositories for rubbish. Post holes also indicate above-ground galleries, which may have been storage for seed-corn. Pairs of post-holes perhaps show the sites of racks, for, perhaps, drying crops.

The huts often have a paved entrance-way, but the floors are of beaten earth, or rubble packed with trodden soil, under which, perhaps for drainage, small flat stones sometimes merged into the subsoil.

Apart from roasting food directly on the hearth, their method of cooking involved a boiling pit, attested by the plentiful finds of boiling stones, known as 'pot boilers'. These were heated on the fire and dropped into a round pit lined with skin, one by one until the water boiled. Willoughby Gardner, writing about Dinorben in Bezant Lowe's *Heart of Northern Wales*, explains that this was the only way available to them to boil water, since "coarse native pottery would not stand the fire, and the good Romano-British imported ware was probably costly" – but why, we wonder, are there no iron cauldrons?

We know what they ate, as has been mentioned, their diet being mixed, of shell-fish and ox meat, and in one case, it seems, the flesh of horses; and from the evidence of their grinding-stones – at first (and almost always in the hillforts) a flat stone with a round one rubbed across it, later, picking up Roman habits, of the rotary type –we know that they made flour. What else, we wonder, did they do, when they were not fighting or subsisting?

The archaeological evidence does throw up some suggestion of ornament, such as a bronze pin of a brooch of the La Tène period, and perhaps fragments of a torque at Penmaenmawr and bronze bracelets, a ring, an ear-ring and a little bronze brooch plated with gold, from Dinorben. But these are exceptional, and for hillfort life in general it seems we must accept the Inventory's opinion that the evidence is that it was conducted under circumstances of extreme austerity, at least until the Roman period.

That life in general had developed to encompass specialisation is evident not only from the existence of a priestly class, but from the fact that pottery was mostly acquired, not locally made. Evidence of Celtic artefacts elsewhere shows us that society was sufficiently sophisticated at the time to value the skills of specialist artists too, that is, people whose task was not to serve survival but to please. The harsh reality of the hillforts is emphasised by the fact that only two pure examples of the work of such a specialist have been found – the cast bronze ox-head ornaments from Dinorben.

One of these remarkable objects was found in 1912, the second (the larger of the two) in 1956. Both are very small, the earlier find measuring only an inch and a half in length, the later two and a half. They are known by the archaeologists as 'escutcheons', which could be any sort of decorative plate, but are thought, by reference to other examples of animal-head plates elsewhere, to have been decorations to the handles of buckets. Possibly of 2nd century origin, the later one being perhaps early 3rd, they both show the distant influence of La Tène style.

The first one found, thought to be the earlier, is greatly more stylised. The eyes are large, oval and oblique. The muzzle of the animal is curved-in sharply at the sides, spreading at the bottom to end in huge flared nostrils. The later one is much more representational, and therefore showing non-Celtic influence. Its face is straighter, its muzzle squared, the nostrils mere pits at the base. Both, however, form part of a long tradition of such artefacts in Britain, and it is known that such pieces were part of the fittings for ceremonial stave-built pails, probably used for carrying milk. The rarity of such work in the hillforts (and their occurrence elsewhere) tells us something, at least, about hillfort life: these were not on the whole the sort of places where there was time for items of luxury or indulgence in appreciation of style and skill or pride in cultural inheritance. The fact of their existence here, however, tells us something we might not otherwise have noticed: such skill was, after all, available here to be indulged in.

You do not often get close to them, these Iron Age ancestors of ours, but when you occasionally do, it seems close indeed. These ox-head bucket-handle-ornaments tell us a wealth of things about the time. You do not, after all, have to ornament a functional item with artistic form, certainly not in so fine a way. We know then that somebody had time and leisure enough to raise their lives to a higher plane, and that they had developed the skills by which to do this.

Preservation of the native way of life was part of the function of the hillforts, though assimilation to the Roman conquest, which is well represented in other parts of Britain, also seems to have gone on here: at Dinorben and elsewhere they used wheel-turned pottery which had an ultimately Roman origin. Nevertheless, there is no doubt that the hillforts came into their own as features of resistance to the Roman advance – a period of repair took place in 55 and 54 BC, on the arrival of Caesar – and that their main period of function was largely over when the Romans won. "Hillfort defences," writes Stanford, in *The Archaeology of the Welsh Marches*, "could not be held for long against Roman siege tactics". Tacitus tells us that Scapula led a campaign against the Deceangli, which perhaps resulted in the removal of the inhabitants of the fort on the Wrekin down to the new town of Wroxeter, just as the population of Maiden Castle had been moved down to Dorchester.

Nothing was thereafter quite the same. Stanford paints a

picture of a concentration of population and an organised chain of command which the Romans had to destroy by dispersing the population, "reducing once proud strongholds to deserted villages", the natives being allowed to go on farming, but now "in fragmented communities, shorn of authority first by defeat and then by isolation".

Certainly anyone who has stood on one of these defiant prominences knows the psychological value attached to the fact of being on top of a hill.

FOUR

TENTATIVE CONCLUSIONS

One of the great debates in the literature is as to whether the hillforts were permanently occupied, or rather places of occasional refuge. Christopher Hawkes, for instance, considers that they would be (mainly) in use 'from time to time' when hostilities broke out. W.J. Varley, writing of the hillforts of the Welsh Marches in the *Archaeological Journal* in 1948, was convinced that the Cheshire hillforts were permanently occupied, but as Stanford says "there is insufficient evidence to indicate the intensity and duration of such settlement", so that it could still be that this 'permanent' occupation took place at widely separated periods. He himself comes to the conclusion that at least some forts, such as Caer Caradoc and the Wrekin, formed permanent settlements. The authors of *Prehistoric Wales* leave open the possibility that the forts, overlooking, as they often are, fertile valleys, "could have functioned not only as refuges for valley-dwellers in times of stress, but also as the social, political and possibly even religious foci of these communities". Stanford also sees them as possibly functioning as meeting places.

The reason all these authorities admit any doubts in the first place is not the lack of evidence for permanent settlement, since it is pointed out (by Hawkes) that cultures relying on wooden or leather utensils, using no pottery, living in timber houses founded on sleeper beams, may leave little trace. It is not that the experts worry about. It is the lack of water.

Seeing a fort as a temporary refuge Hawkes points out "helps to explain what has puzzled so many people, the absence of a water-supply inside most hill-forts. Regular sieges were plainly undreamed of, and there would normally be nothing to interfere with the fetching of water from a source outside the defences, and often indeed far below them, as it is fetched by the dwellers in the modern hill-forts of Algeria". In the 1904 report on the huts of Tre'r Ceiri, for instance, it is explained that the only water available was that which gathers on the peaty soil of the hut floors, which would (it is judged) "be quite inadequate for the needs of any considerable number of men and animals". A small supply exists a few hundred yards north of the outer north-west entrance. The conclusion that "Tre'r Ceiri was a strong refuge, into which the inhabitants of the surrounding neighbourhood could retire with their flocks and herds and household belongings, and there remain until the temporary danger had passed" also helps to explain the lack of finds.

Hawkes, referring to Algerian villages, had an earlier article in *Antiquity* in mind, 'Algerian Hill-forts of today', written by M. W. Hilton-Simpson, published in the edition of December 1927. Hilton-Simpson says water from the stream below was carried up daily in goatskins by women. Hence, the hillfort would be unable to withstand a siege. "This lack of water storage, in a country thoroughly accustomed to a state of war, has always been a mystery to me…" He concludes that short raids were all that were to be expected.

Similar conclusions (which would also have been available to Hawkes) were published in the March 1927 edition of the same journal, in an article called 'Maori Hill-Forts', by Raymond Firth. Here again in siege conditions "the weak point was usually lack of water. As a rule the hill-fort had no spring within it, and anyone venturing out to get water was cut off by the besiegers". It is, of course, an inbuilt problem which comes with the very advantage of elevation to which the fort owes its strength. Dyer (in *Hillforts of England and Wales*) concludes that siege warfare was not the norm – until the Romans came. "This suggests that attacks on forts were expected to be short and sharp, with no prolonged siege in which lack of water would have resulted in the fort's downfall." The well reported at Penmaenmawr comes to seem of some significance.

Elsewhere, experts have posited other functions for the enclosures – the storage of grain, the location of markets – and in the examples of stone hillforts in Tennessee in the United States, the sacred enclosure of a ceremonial site. The booklet published by the University of Tennessee on the subject of the 'Old Stone Fort' on the Duck River, for instance, argues from the lack of debris that "If the enclosures were built to be occupied in time of danger, some of them were apparently never needed". Lack of litter is compatible with a ritual site, such always being kept clean. We have, however, in Wales, the evidence of the sling stones for at least a part of their use.

Of course we do not have to come down firmly in favour of any one conclusion. It is argued, in *Prehistoric Wales*, that "It is most unlikely that all hillforts functioned in the same way on either a temporal or spatial basis, even within well-defined geographical zones". In favour of the ritual aspect, Hogg cites the legend of Dinas Emrys, which connects human sacrifice with a hillfort, for which there is also evidence at Maiden Castle and Hod Hill.

There is one feature of the northern Wales hillforts to which I have, in passing, drawn attention. This is their mutual inter-visibility. To generalise (and perhaps there are exceptions): from each of them you can see at least one more in at least two directions. The fact that this feature could be part of their use does not, of course, provide proof of the conclusion that it was their main function. But consider: if each of these hilltops had a beacon on it, that would only have to be manned by a small garrison. That would explain the lack of huts, in many cases, and the general scarcity of finds. The chain of visibility would then work like a semaphore system, such as did indeed, at one time, run from Holyhead to Liverpool.

Thus, something observed from Caer y Twr, on Holyhead Mountain, or from Castell Odo, at the end of Llŷn, could be conveyed as information along the coastal chain to reach Pen y Corddyn within a few minutes – very much faster than a raiding party could travel – and from there flow on down the Clwyd valley or on to the Cheshire and Shropshire hills. This would have two effects, at once. It would enable a settled farming community to carry on its business in the fertile valleys below the hillforts, in the knowledge that nobody is going to take them by surprise and that (being always within sight of a beacon) they can at any time go up to the hillfort of their particular community to take refuge. Secondly, it would mean that by the time the raiders reached the valleys there was nothing there for them to take, which would, in the long run, prove a disincentive to their coming at all.

An expanding, settled farming population in the valleys below could also explain the sheer number of the forts. Each group, perhaps extended family, sub-clan, or whatever, would need to have their own, or there would not be room. Such a system would not work so well without the use of a chain of signals. Without that, there would not be time – when the raiding parties arrived in your valley – to get everything into the secure fold of the protected area. With it in place, however, you would be well ahead of them. Being on a hilltop with far-reaching views is of course a half in itself. In places historically plagued by pirates – such as the eastern Aegean in medieval times – hilltop living was the adopted norm. Thus, on many Greek islands the population lived, all the time, in a secure summit village, until recent times.

Nothing one says now on the subject of the hillforts can be original, so much discussion having already taken place, and I know that this tentative hypothesis is far from new. Hogg says that much attention was paid in the early part of the last century to the intervisibility of the hillforts, but that there is nothing remarkable about this feature: "...hill-tops can usually be seen from other hill-tops, and it has never been demonstrated that the number of fortified sites visible one from another is greater than would occur by chance". There are ways in which these ideas could be tested, he goes on, but "until that has been done they must be dismissed as unproven speculations". 'Dismissed' one could quarrel with; unproven they may be, but that would perhaps encourage an attempt to prove them, not dismiss them. Hogg says the site choice was governed only by the need to defend a place with the least expenditure of work. Yet it seems likely to have included elements of more significance, and we have noticed again and again the proximity to the sites of forts of fertile land.

Much of what we know of the way of life which gave rise to the hillforts is gained, not by direct evidence, but by inference, by the sling-stones and burnt gateways indicating occasional, perhaps habitual, states of war; by the ox-head ornaments indicating a successful agricultural society as in which that specialisation could occur, since skilled craftsmen have to be paid some way, for instance by being fed through the efforts of others. And since somebody has to arrange all this, we have to suppose a politico-economic structure also being in place. The values this is based on have to be agreed, by means of some code of conduct, or it would not work. So a whole structure of exchange between aesthetic and economic demands has to be in place as well, one type of value being balanced against another in the eternal social equation.

Such factors may be rare, but they are there. Day to day life is better attested by the rubbish-dumps of ox bones and seafood shells, and the residue of the other aspects of their daily lives.

What we know mainly, though, since it is the best-known thing about the Iron Age, is that they built these hill-top look-outs overlooking the land they farmed – something, at this long stretch away, for which I am so much indebted to them, these distant predecessors, for giving me not just this chance to try to understand them better, but also to appreciate now again the quality of the country which I have seen, theirs and ours, in the enjoyable course of writing this book.

Note

There are hundreds of hillforts even within the limited area chosen here, and I have only been able to deal in this book with a fairly random (but I hope representative) sample. This has been partly limited by the information available. Some recent work is still continuing, and a book such as this has to be a historical retrospective rather than an up-to-date report, since the nature of that would change year by year.

ACKNOWLEDGEMENTS

The author would like particularly to thank Frances Lynch for her invaluable guidance and information; Tom Parry, for providing a copy of his translation of an article; and, as usual, the staff at Conwy Library for their more than conscientious efforts, which have been so much a help in the work of research.

BIBLIOGRAPHY

ALCOCK, Leslie. *Castell Odo: an embanked settlement on Mynydd Ystum, near Aberdaron, Caernarvonshire.* Archaeologia Cambrensis. Vol CIX-CX. 1960-61

CAESAR, Julius. Trs. Handford, S.A. *The Conquest of Gaul.* Penguin, London, 1951.

CUNLIFFE, Barry. *Iron Age Communities in Britain.* Routledge & Kegan Paul, London, 1978.

DODD, A.N. (ed.) *A History of Wrexham.* Hughes & Son, Wrexham, 1957.

DOWSON, A.H. *Ordnance Survey Map of Southern Britain in the Iron Age.* Southampton, 1967.

DYER, James. *Hillforts of England and Wales.* Shire Publications Ltd., Buckinghamshire, 2003.

FIRTH, Raymond. *Maori Hill-Forts.* Antiquity, Vol. I No.1. March 1927.

GARDNER, Willoughby, and Savory H.N. *Dinorben.* National Museum of Wales, Cardiff, 1964.

HAWKES, Christopher. *Hill-Forts – A Retrospect.* Antiquity, Vol. V. No. 17. March 1931.

HILTON-SIMPSON, M.W. *Algerian Hill-Forts of Today.* Antiquity, Vol. I No.IV. December, 1927.

HOGG, A.H.A. *Hill-Forts of Britain.* Hart-Davies, London, 1975. *Garn Boduan and Tre'r Ceiri, Excavations at two Caernarvonshire Hill-Forts.* Archaeological Journal, 117, 1960.

HOULDER, Christopher. *Rescue Excavations at Moel Hiraddug.* Flintshire Historical Society Publications , Vol. 19, 1961.

JONES, Rev. Owen. *Pen Dinas.* 1875. Trs. Tom Parry, 1992. Private paper.

LOWE, W. Bezant. *The Heart of Northern Wales.* Vol. I, 1912. Vol. II 1927. Llanfairfechan.

LYNCH, Frances. *Prehistoric Wales.* Sutton Publishing, Stroud, 2000.

PENNANT, Thomas. *Tours in Wales.* Vol. III. H. Humphreys, Caernarvon, 1883.

ROYAL COMMISSION *on Ancient and Historical Monuments in Wales and Monmouthshire.* Inventories for Caernarvonshire (3 vols.) and Anglesey. HMSO, 1956, 1960, 1964, 1968.

SENIOR, Michael. *Disputed Border.* Gwasg Carreg Gwalch, Llanrwst, 1989.
North Wales in the Making. Ibid.,1995.

STANFORD, S.C. *The Archaeology of the Welsh Marches.* Collins, London, 1980.

TACITUS, *On Britain and Germany.* Trs. Mattingly, H. Penguin, London, 1948.

WILLIAMS, Rev. Robert. *The History and Antiquities of the Town of Aberconwy and its Neighbourhood.* Thomas Gee, Denbigh, 1835.

WILSON, H.L. *Llandudno and District in Line and Legend.* (Publisher unknown).